To
Ellen Elizabeth Spong
Mary Katharine Spong
Jaquelin Ketner Spong
Augustus Charles Epps, Jr.
John Baldwin Catlett, Jr.

. . . daughters and sons-in-law who expanded my life
and into whose hands I am content to place the
destiny of both the church and the world

Contents

Foreword

The Book of Acts opens with an account of a critical decision made by the new community of the people who accepted Jesus as Lord. The decision had to do with the necessary qualifications of the person selected to replace Judas. Plainly these people had no truck with the various personality inventories of that time. There is no deference to any standard for "I.Q.," no required credit rating. Their only stipulation was, "One of the men who have accompanied us during all the time that the Lord Jesus went in and out among us, beginning from the baptism of John until the day when he was taken up from us—one of these men must become with us a witness to his resurrection" (Acts 1:21–22, RSV). As the record indicates, the apostles selected Matthias by the power of the Holy Spirit. In so doing, they placed an "indelible dimension" into all future Christian witness. So significant did the earliest Christians regard this "indelible dimension" that Paul, from whom the earliest New Testament account of the resurrection emanates, could declare, "If Christ has not been raised, then our preaching is in vain and your faith is in vain" (1 Corinthians 15:14). It is about the reality and the power of this "indelible dimension" that Bishop John J. Spong writes so persuasively and so honestly in *The Easter Moment*.

Bishop Spong is one of those rare people that the Episcopal Church—complex and baffling as it sometimes is—spawns in the ranks of its ordained ministry, eventually blossoming brilliantly and ably in its House of Bishops. Robert Mackie of Scotland in a tribute to the late W. A. Visser't Hooft, the World Council of Churches' founding General Secretary, wrote, "He was a Christian with a lively mind who was prepared to do the hard work necessary for the realization of some of his dreams." *The Easter Moment*, as do other of Bishop Spong's books, lectures, and sermons, plainly indicates that the essence of such a tribute is applicable to him also.

Descriptive of Bishop Spong's competence and resourcefulness also could be Dr. Vesser't Hooft's observation about Karl Barth, after being persuaded by a friend to read the second edition of *Epistle to the Romans* (1923): "I found it a terribly difficult book, but I did understand enough to become deeply impressed . . . here was a man who lived in the modern world, . . . a man who struggled with the problems of historical criticism and of modern philosophy—but who had rediscovered the authority of the word of God. This was a man who proclaimed the death of all the little comfortable gods and spoke again of the living God of the Bible" (*The Christian Century*, July 1985, p. 669).

In *The Easter Moment*, Bishop Spong deals with the resurrection event pastorally, sharing with readers the profoundly moving and illuminating experience of ministering to and being ministered to by a friend, a young and able physician who was dying of a rare, incurable disease. Bishop Spong grapples with the resurrection event by examining the testimony of the earliest traditions that embrace it, treating the sources objectively in the mode of modern biblical criticism. He carefully assesses hypotheses associated with the empty tomb and the absence of a dead body. He refuses to be intimidated by the difficult questions. As author Spong observes, "The moment of Easter appears to be subjective at some points, objective at others, but essentially it is always beyond both categories" (p. 139). "Every description is inevitably a distortion, but that distortion does not mean that the event being described was not real. Easter was a ringing confirmation that beyond the limit of our eyes, or the touch of our hands, there was an eternal, timeless reality" (p. 168).

The burden of proof concerning the resurrection and its consequences is carried first by the conclusion that it is only to the "eyes of faith" that such reality embodied in *The Easter Moment* becomes convincing and therefore efficacious for human life. "That risen Christ was real. I cannot say that too emphatically. He was not resuscitated, he was resurrected. He was changed. It was not the limited physical eyes of our humanity that saw him, but eyes of faith newly opened by the power of his life" (p. 196). And second, the burden of proof is carried by the miraculous change that the reality of the resurrection wrought in the little band of despairing, fearful, disillusioned, hopeless post-Good Friday followers of Jesus, for it transformed them into a formidable community of believers in the risen Christ whose total commitment "would start a movement that would transform the world" (p. 197).

John Elbridge Hines
Highlands, North Carolina
Presiding Bishop
The Episcopal Church
1964–1974

Preface
to the Second Edition

Perhaps the greatest joy an author can know comes from the necessity of writing the preface to a new edition of a previously published book. *The Easter Moment* was originally published in April of 1980. Since that date this book, like all books, has developed a life of its own. It has been used in congregational study groups and at summer conferences in such places as Kanuga in western North Carolina, Chautauqua Institute in western New York, Camp Galilee at Lake Tahoe, Nevada, and the Episcopal Conference Center in Cove, Oregon. It has also been used by judicatory gatherings of clergy for continuing education. I have conducted lecture series based on this book for clergy of the Methodist, Episcopal, and Mar Thoma traditions in such places as New Jersey, Texas, Virginia, Oklahoma, and far away India.

Since the first publication of this book I have

continued to read in the field of biblical scholarship, especially as it pertains to the experience of Easter. I have been particularly moved by the work of Edward Schillebeeckx in his book *Jesus* and by the writing of Pheme Perkins in her book *Resurrection: New Testament and Contemporary Reflections*. Though these two authors have expanded my knowledge, they have not caused me to shift my conclusions in a significant way. My original work on *The Easter Moment* also launched me beyond the narrow focus of that book into a study of the whole question of life after death. This study has engaged my scholarly attention since 1980 and should find expression in another book in the not-too-distant future. I hope to trace the power of the idea of life after death throughout history, to seek to understand the human anxiety to which that idea speaks, and to discover how that anxiety is met when life after death fades in the consciousness of the people as I think it has faded in our century. I also hope to discover new words and concepts that might lead us to look at this possibility in a fresh way. It has been revealing for me to isolate the eschatological concepts in particular faith traditions such as Judaism, Christianity, Islam, Hinduism, and Buddhism. Such an experience produces the surprising conclusion that there is no fixed content in regard to life after death in any religious tradition, including Christianity. Life after death is an idea that has grown and changed over the years in every faith system. Few believers, however, give much evidence of being consciously aware of this development.

To move beyond the assumptions of one's own belief system to engage another religious viewpoint in meaningful dialogue requires a ready knowledge and a mastery of the nuances of one's faith. Before considering life after death in general, life after death in the specific Christian understanding is essential. *The Easter Moment* attempts to take the insights of biblical scholars related to the Easter event and make them both available to and understandable by the average man or woman who occupies the pews of our churches. I remain convinced that the leadership of the Christian church regularly insults the intelligence of the laity by trying to protect them from the commonly accepted work of scholars, thereby refusing to let them worship God with their minds. The day has long passed when lay people will accept religious propositions simply on the authority of the church or of scripture. Such propositions must stand in their own compelling integrity and be capable of competing effectively in the common quest for truth. For the church to offer its lay people no alternatives except the choice between various literal accounts of critical moments in our Christian story and the complete rejection of those accounts is to guarantee a church whose only members will be those who either cannot or will not think for themselves.

The Easter Moment will challenge those who want to be fundamentalistic about the words of the Bible describing Easter. If my mail is an accurate reflection of people's response, it will create anger among the religiously insecure. Its purpose, however, is not to do that but to open new vistas on theological truth to those for whom the literalizations have become empty words. My hope is that this book will lead modern men and women to make powerful religious commitments without having to deny the insights of their own generation. For that group whose name is legion, and among whom I locate my own grown daughters, this book is written.

I am pleased that this new edition carries with it a foreword by the Right Reverend John Elbridge Hines, former Presiding Bishop of the Episcopal Church. This man, long my friend, mentor, colleague, and role model, led our church through the turbulent decade of urban riots and Vietnam with such authenticity that he is remembered today, more than a decade after his retirement, as a crucial figure in American church history. During his active career he maintained a rather conservative theological position for himself personally, but he had the vision to enable him to allow others to press the theological edges and to create in the Episcopal Church the flexibility to support that kind of theological frontiersmanship. It was his leadership that in many ways made my particular ministry possible. I am enormously in his debt.

I repeat here my gratitude to the clergy and people of the Diocese of Newark for encouraging me to pursue the scholar-bishop style of episcopacy and for inviting me to share my exploratory theological journey with them in regularly scheduled lectures, and to my brothers (regrettably, at this moment there are no sisters) in the House of Bishops who have in significant ways affirmed my rather unique vocation in this office. I especially refer to the Rt. Rev. Rustin Kimsey of Eastern Oregon, the Rt. Rev. Wesley Frensdorff of Arizona, the Rt. Rev. Edmond Browning of Hawaii, the Rt. Rev. Herbert Donovan of Arkansas, and to four of our now-retired bishops who have been special friends in this enterprise: the Rt. Rev. William Spofford, the Rt. Rev. William H. Marmion, the Rt. Rev. George Murray, and the Rt. Rev. Robert F. Gibson.

I would also like to acknowledge my appreciation to the community of Point O' Woods, New York, and to the people at Good Shepherd Church in Cashiers, North Carolina, where I have been privileged to spend parts of the summer in residence as a writer.

Finally, I wish to thank those who assisted me in both the original as well as this new edition of this book. In Richmond, Virginia, that list includes Lucy Newton Boswell Negus, Carter Donnan McDowell, Frank Eakin, Eleanor Freed Evans, and Ruth Campbell Taylor. Ruth is the widow of Dr. James Campbell, to whom the reader will shortly be introduced.

In Newark those to whom mention is due include Mabel Wynne Allen, Denise G. Haines, James William Henry Sell, Christine Bridger Barney, and John H. Zinn, who either are or have been members of the staff of the Diocese of Newark. They have supported and assisted me in many ways as I try to combine my career as a bishop with my vocation as an author. My special gratitude also goes to Wanda Corwin Hollenbeck, whose warm personality, even temperament, and talent at a word processor were particularly helpful in preparing this new edition for publication, and to Robert Lanterman, John Grady, Olga Hayes, Dorothy Lynch, Barbara Lescota, Margaret Allenspach, Jean Stufflebeem, Gail Deckenbach, Elizabeth Stone, Calvin Sylvester, and Janis Daley, all of whom make Cathedral House such a pleasant place in which to work.

Finally, I thank my family: Joan, my wife; Ellen, Katharine, and Jaquelin, now my grown, quite independent and career-oriented daughters; and Gus Epps and Jack Catlett, who have entered my life as sons-in-law and who, with my daughters, give this father an incredible amount of emotional support. I previously acknowledged Hermann, our cat, but he now rests in peace beneath a holly tree at our home in New Jersey.

Life is a portrait with sunshine and shadow. I enjoy it immensely because there are such wonderful people with whom I share it. It is out of the joy of life that I anticipate dimensions of that life that death cannot conquer.

Part I

A Personal Witness

Chapter 1

An Autobiographical Word

Is it possible to believe that Easter is real? Can a child of the twentieth century with any integrity be a part of a community of faith that rests on the affirmation that one named Jesus of Nazareth some two thousand years ago did, in fact, break the power of death? Can it be asserted today with any credibility that there is life after death? Or are these but fond hopes and pious dreams that emotionally weak people create because they cannot tolerate the vision of nothingness that death seems to be?

I am a Christian. I do not believe it is possible to be a Christian without saying yes to Easter, yes to resurrection, and yes to life after death. I am also a person who has been shaped and formed by my generation. I am the product of the evangelical Bible Belt of the South in whose fundamentalist tradition no miracle of the Bible is too spectacular to be accepted on faith. But in my life that religious heritage has been challenged, eroded, and finally abandoned under pressure from the secular spirit of modern education, the scientific revolution, and the pervasive skepticism of my age. I constantly struggle to shape the form of those things I passionately believe so that I can meet head-on the doubt that my generation constantly engenders.

The result of this attempt on my part to bridge these two worlds is frequently that the *defender of the faith* types are not certain that I believe enough, while the *modern, religiously emancipated* types are quite certain that I am a naïve, old-fashioned believer who only pretends to be part of the twentieth century. I see myself, not surprisingly, as in neither camp. Rather, I believe I am one who is convinced of the truth of the Christian faith, but I am also convinced that this truth lies beyond the religious forms that we use in our attempt to convey that truth. I cannot literalize any of those forms, whether they be the Bible, the creeds, or the sacred traditions.

To illustrate this, let me state that I believe in the reality of God. That is the personal center of my deepest conviction. But I think every attempt to define what we mean by God is finally inadequate and must be seen as such by its adherents. (Some attempts are more inadequate than others.) I believe that in the life of Jesus of Nazareth God has uniquely and decisively entered human history, but I do not believe a definitive Christology has yet been formulated. Even the Chalcedonian formula[1], which is the definitive Christological formula, says more about who the Christ is not than about who the Christ is. Chalcedon really set the parameters within which the Christological debate could be waged.

Finally, as this book will reveal, I believe that the Moment of Easter was real. I am convinced that Jesus tested the ultimate human barrier of death and penetrated it in a way that not only affects me but is decisive for me. Yet, I am also certain that the words we use to describe that Moment are woefully inadequate vehicles to convey the wonder and the power to which they point. When analyzing the theological forms and the biblical narratives, I can be as skeptical as anyone. When I get past those forms and narratives and experience the reality to which they point, I can be as rhapsodic as any believer. This is a delicate but all-important distinction.

My life experience in the priesthood has convinced me that the church does not take seriously enough the doubts, fears, and questions of lay people. The church acts so often as if we are still in the thirteenth century, when only the priest was educated and all of the lay people were willing to believe on the authority of the church alone. In the thirteenth century the priest would tell the people what to believe, and they would respond by believing it. Many a clergyman today tries to play the same game. This may seem like a caricature, but it is accurate more times than I would like to believe.

The cumulative result is that the more educated the laity, the more the church has faded as a major factor in the intellectual life of Western civilization. The issues that theologians debate hardly cause a ripple in the secular city unless they relate to a current secular issue such as the women's movement or the sexual revolution.

The churches that I have served as rector and the diocese that I now serve as bishop have been willing to be something different. They have opted for a searching, probing theological journey. They have encouraged doubt that delves beneath the surface, questions that cry out to be answered. They have been places where the deepest scholarship that is Christian has interacted with scholarship from other disciplines in a relentless search for truth.

When the vocation to journey theologically into the exciting and insecure unknown is grasped by the church, the response has always been incredible. Belief that emerges at the end of an honest inquiry has an integrity that the old authoritarianism never possessed. But when one allows doubt or heresy to be articulated inside the community of faith, one must be prepared to listen to the threat levels of those who cannot deal with uncertainty. It will be loud and frequent.

I can give my personal testimony that for me the rewards of this kind of searching openness have been deeply enriching. I can honestly say that the more I probe the Christian story, the more deeply I believe it to be true. There have been for me moments of sheer ecstasy in my pilgrimage. Sight has faded into insight, and insight into new vision. Conviction has grown about things that are essential, while external things have fallen aside.

Nothing has ever captured my attention more deeply than the Moment of Easter. Death entered my life early. My grandfather died when I was three. I asked for an explanation, and my mother's response was filled with her natural piety and literal images of heaven. It was not her intention, I am certain, but her explanation filled me with more fear than faith; for the God she sought to portray as a kind, heavenly Father came across as a capricious authority figure who snatched away little boys' grandfathers out of his need for companionship. This experience merely heightened my sense that somehow this God must be placated and obeyed. Why this God should be loved I could not imagine.

When I was twelve my father died. So little was he involved in church that his funeral was held at home. I was not allowed to go. Somehow the experience was thought to be too difficult for me. Once again, my mother's desire to protect me had exactly the opposite effect. My vision of death was filled with a fearful and negative mystery. My own feelings about my father's death were never dealt with by anyone. Again, I got pious platitudes that begged above all not to be questioned, for they were offered with a kind of sentimentality that betrayed the embarrassment of phoniness. I had begun that inevitable process of adolescent rebellion, and my relationship with my father was far from satisfactory at that moment. His death only filled me with unresolved guilt and unanswered questions that I would deal with unconsciously in my behavior patterns and personality development for years. The fact that I made these things conscious in psychotherapy years later gave me insight but unfortunately not freedom from many of the debilitations and scars of that death experience.

My next confrontation with death did not come until shortly after ordination, when I began to realize existentially that a major portion of my newly chosen profession was to deal with death and dying. Despite some training in pastoral theology, it all seemed academic until the time came to plan my first funeral service. Then it became painfully obvious that I needed to be honest about what I believed and to act upon that belief with integrity. I could not parrot empty theological clichés or meaningless pious words. These empty gestures had never meant anything to me and I had no reason to think they would be meaningful to anyone else. I had to know what I believed, and I had to believe whatever I said. My life as a priest demanded that

I search as deeply as I could into the meaning of life after death.

I was discovering the remarkable fact that for my pastoral ministry it was the Easter Moment that loomed as all-important. The critical moment in the entire Christian faith had now emerged as the critical moment in my own personal pastoral ministry. The realization of this fact meant that I had to devote my time to an exploration of that moment. I have done so for twenty-five years now. This book is the fruit of that study.

There were some high points in the pilgrimage. In 1957 when I was a young priest, I was invited to join the summer staff at Kanuga, the major Episcopal conference center in the South. Kanuga is located in the beautiful pine-covered mountains of western North Carolina. The keynote speaker for the adult conference that summer was the dean of the Theological Seminary of the University of the South at Sewanee, Tennessee, George M. Alexander, a man who was later to become the Bishop of Upper South Carolina and my good friend. At the last minute an emergency prevented Dean Alexander from attending, and I was asked to fill in as his substitute. The material I had already prepared for a small seminar at Kanuga became the major lectures at the conference. Each day that week, for the first time publicly, I shared my thoughts on the Resurrection.

The response was enormously encouraging. It was my first major lecture experience, and the response convinced me that the subject of resurrection and life after death touched chords deep in the psyche of every person. This encouraged me to dig deeper and deeper into this subject.

I began to search for books that would illumine this

area of my life and faith. There were surprisingly few, enabling me to read every one I could find. More often than not they were not helpful. When written by believers, they tried to prove too much. When written by nonbelievers, they seemed content with too little. However, I poured my most creative energies into my study of the Resurrection.

In 1968 I took a mini-sabbatical from my parish duties in Lynchburg, Virginia, and went to Yale. There I worked in the Divinity School library exclusively on the subject of the Resurrection—probing, searching out leads, driving ever deeper into and beyond the scriptures. And there I first discovered the writings of Wolfhart Pannenberg, and at that moment his was the best voice I heard speaking on the subject. But that opinion did not last, for I came to find Pannenburg almost too literal, too historic. If Easter had been as he suggested, then there was no reason why all people did not acknowledge Jesus as risen and worship him as Lord. Since obviously they did not, why were *they* unconvinced?

While serving as rector of St. Paul's Church in Richmond, two new books came to my attention and forced me to redo all of my resurrection material in the light of what I learned from them. These were Norman Perrin's remarkable little book, *The Resurrection Tradition in Matthew, Mark, and Luke,* and Reginald Fuller's brilliant work, *The Formation of the Resurrection Narratives.* Both books opened many doors for me, through which I walked quite eagerly. I did a new sermon series in Richmond during the Easter season of 1974 in which these fresh learnings were incorporated. Another step towards this book had been taken. It was still not enough.

The next step was my relationship with Dr. James

Campbell, which I shall discuss in detail in the next chapter. Suffice it to say here that dealing with this man and his death forced me to filter everything I had learned intellectually into the reality of human experience. The circle was almost complete.

In 1976 I was elected bishop, and in the spring of 1977 I was asked to deliver a lecture series to the clergy of the Diocese of Newark on the subject of "The Resurrection." I accepted and brought this lifetime of study to a new level of both intensity and preparation. Since that time I have led the clergy conferences in two other dioceses and conducted teaching missions in five congregations with lay people on this subject. I have also been blessed with another treasured book, Hans Küng's *On Being a Christian*. This book has served to confirm and validate much of my pilgrimage. His insights into the Resurrection deepened and clarified my own. At least I felt ready to share my years of study on this subject.

My search will not end here. This book will be offered to the church at large, and in reaction I will learn more, and my thought may deepen or even change. But even if the way I understand or articulate the meaning of Easter changes, I do believe I have touched a reality and experienced a moment that will not change. In this volume I will seek to lead my reader to that reality beyond my words and my concepts.

I invite you to journey into that Easter Moment. I will be your guide as far as I can go.

Chapter 2

A Look through Death

This will be a personal volume, for beyond all my study it was the life and death of a person that brought this book together for me. His name was Jim Campbell. Because I knew Jim, I had a new way of looking at Jesus and new eyes to begin to see the meaning of resurrection. To share with my readers my understanding of the Easter Moment demands that I also share the story of Jim Campbell.

I have been a privileged man, privileged to know and to share life with a significant number of people. I mean nothing superficial by that statement, for to know another, to share life with another, is a profound, a rare, and an expanding experience. Most of us spend our lives erecting security systems that keep anyone from knowing our deepest thoughts, our innermost being. The mystery of our own personhood is for many, perhaps for most, locked forever in secret chambers and frequently hidden even from ourselves.

Our generation has witnessed an explosion of consciousness that probes the inner self. Depth psychology explores territory that few even a hundred years ago could have imagined. Yoga, meditation, group therapy, and even the use of hallucinogenic drugs find much of their appeal in their promise to introduce one to oneself. People have felt the need of these aids because without them few people can risk exposing themselves to another person. I suppose we all fear that if anyone gets to know us as well as we know ourselves, they might judge us as harshly as we judge ourselves. Self-negativity is an enormously powerful force at work in the human psyche.

But when you allow another to enter your life, to know your deepest self, to share that personal mystery, even to accept that darker side of your existence, it is a powerful, a moving, and a life-changing moment. We yearn for this depth of community with another even though we fear it.

The deepest joy of being an ordained minister for me has been those relationships where I was privileged to get beneath the protective barriers, to meet the real person who lives underneath those barriers, to experience a depth of life that I think is rare, to perceive a quality of life that few ever know. The rarest of all such relationships has come in my ministry to the dying. The one relationship that I treasure above all else and from which I learned the most about life and death and life beyond death was with Jim Campbell, a particular dying person. I can honestly say that I met this man more deeply than I have ever met another human being. He and his life illumined the subject of this book very specifically.

In the summer of 1975 I vacationed with my family on the exquisite Outer Banks of North Carolina. Returning to my parish the last of August, I went through a list of routine notices entitled "while you were away," which had been prepared for me by my administrative assistant. They were designed to bring to my attention quickly anything that I needed to know or that I needed to follow up. In the midst of the list I read "Jim Campbell went to the hospital to check some swelling in his feet. They think it is an allergic reaction to a fertilizer he has been using on his roses." I called Jim at home to check. He repeated the remark about the allergy, but there was a tone about his voice that belied the confidence his words were trying to convey. I asked if I could come over that evening. He said, "Fine," and at 8:00 P.M. I arrived at his house.

Jim Campbell was an anesthesiologist in Richmond, Virginia. He had been confirmed in my parish about a year before. His wife, Ruth, who was a pediatrician, had long been a member, as were their son, John, and their daughter, Elizabeth, who were eleven and eight years of age, respectively. Jim was forty-four, a man of many interests: music, literature, genealogy, and roses among them. He had a deceptive shyness about him that was winsome. He had countless friends.

Jim had been president of his medical school class at the Medical College of Virginia. He had not gone directly to medical school after college and consequently was a bit older than his classmates. This was a crucial fact in his life, for he met his wife, Ruth, while in medical school. She was one of his professors. They had done quite well, and both Jim and Ruth were well respected professionally. The arrival of their children required Ruth to curtail her practice, but Jim's career soared. This was an attractive, successful family much admired, perhaps even envied, by those who knew them. My relationship with them at that moment was cordial, friendly, but rather superficial. I had, for example, never been in their house before that evening.

Ruth met me at the door and ushered me to an upstairs sitting room where Jim, clad in pajamas and a robe, was sitting. There was an anxiety in Ruth's face that belied the cavalier quality of her words. She left Jim and me alone, and we had the first significant conversation of our lives. Jim was clinging to the possibility that his body was having a severe allergic reaction, but he said there were other more devastating possibilities, the worst of which was an unusual kind of leukemia. The blood work at the hospital had revealed rather strange data that did not fit into recognizable categories, but it was ominous.

Jim's physicians were also his friends and colleagues, and it was clearly difficult for them to separate their emotions from their practice of medicine. Doctors often seem to be strangely incapable of dealing with mortality, and this was clearly heightened when the patient was their colleague. They decided that Jim should go to Duke Hospital in Durham, North Carolina, for a thorough and objective workup. That maneuver proved to be a smokescreen to cover the fact that none of them could bring themselves to tell Jim what all of them, including Jim himself, knew. I asked Jim if I might go to Duke with him. It was a premature request that was not appropriate to the relationship we had at that moment. He declined my offer, but he did know I was willing to stay with him no matter what the diagnosis might indicate.

I stayed about two hours that first evening. I got him to explain all the options from the best to the worst. He did so with clinical skill and objectivity. When the most dreaded possibility was discussed, my medical knowledge was enhanced, and my insight into the nature of this remarkable man was heightened. When that evening was over, he and I both knew what the diagnosis was, and we also knew that we would be able to talk about it, live with it, and share it. For Jim, having watched in loneliness as his medical friends could not enter this experience with him, there was in our meeting that evening the promise of community that would dramatically shape both of our lives.

Jim and Ruth went to Durham the next day prepared to stay three or four days for an exhaustive medical workup and a firm diagnosis. They returned in one day. The Duke doctors did a bone marrow scan and a bloodsmear, which, coupled with the test results he brought with him, were considered quite sufficient for a full diagnosis. They announced the name that could only have been heard as a death sentence: acute myelomonoblastic leukemia. Cure or even remission of this disease is practically unknown.[2] The treatment is almost as bad as the disease. Many victims of this disease elect to die quickly rather than to struggle with the side effects of the various therapies available, none of which, either singly or in combination, could prolong life beyond a year. But resignation might be easier for some than for this man who was young, vibrant, a happy husband, a needed and loving father, and at the very height of his career capabilities.

I called Jim in Durham shortly after he had received the word. He told me the news with a calm voice. We agreed to meet the next night when he returned to Richmond.

That visit also lasted about two hours. It had elements of all of the stages Dr. Elizabeth Kubler-Ross suggests that dying people go through: rejection, fighting, resignation, denying, hoping, grieving. Jim recapitulated all of these emotions. The diagnosis removed all pretense from our relationship. All of the superficialities were swept aside.

We shared the images we both had of each other from the time we first met, and we laughed about them. We talked about the effects his illness would have on his wife, the children, and his mother. We talked about the impact the treatment would have on him as a person. Some of the side effects were dreadful: loss of hair, violent nausea, impotence, lesions of the mouth. Conversation flowed easily. It set the tone for almost a year that we were to know each other before his death.

As those days went by, revelation followed revelation. Jim shared with me difficult moments from his childhood, his adolescence. Painful experiences that he had tried to forget were called up, relived, perhaps healed. I, in turn, was freed to open my hurtful moments to him. The joys, the successes of both our lives were also shared. There was no sense of embarrassment, for we were free of that human need to inflate the ego.

Jim did not realize it for a while, but he would never practice medicine again in his life. Never did he get well enough to work a full day, and the insurance coverage that he had to carry made part-time work economically unfeasible. When that did dawn on him, it was a foretaste of the death experience itself; for far more than any of us realizes, we receive a great measure of our sense of self-worth from our productive labor. In the practice of medicine, the line between one's personal self and one's professional medical self is always blurred. Jim had immense manual dexterity that found outlets in playing the piano and, interestingly enough, in his ability to type. This latter skill provided the means whereby our lives, his and mine, became even more involved.

Our church was a beehive of activity and consequently was always understaffed. Jim came by often enough to be aware of this and suggested that he might assist in the office. In a few weeks we became the only church I have ever heard of with a physician working as a parish secretary.

Everyone on our staff knew Jim's story. He was able to discuss it freely. They also came to love this incredible man who could enjoy life so deeply and make them enjoy it on levels they had never before imagined. This was his gift to them.

Jim's work in the parish office meant that I saw him daily. Frequently we would find moments to talk about life as we had and were experiencing it. On more than one occasion in my counseling ministry, I met a situation where medical expertise was needed. I would ask my counselees if they would be willing to discuss their problem with a doctor on our staff. They always were willing and I would send them in to see Jim. He was a marvelous pastor; not once did they suspect the incomprehensible drama that they were sharing.

At that time there was a gradual decline, periods of hospitalization, and dreadful treatments, but Jim embraced them all and allowed me to share them with him. I in turn invited him into my life, which at that time involved exciting new dimensions. I was participating in a series of medical ethics dialogues with Dr. Daniel Gregory, a professor of internal medicine at the

Medical College of Virginia, which were later published as a monograph under the title *Life Approaches Death*. Jim was my enormously helpful consultant.

I was also being considered for nomination and *possible* election as bishop coadjutor of Newark, New Jersey, an opportunity about which I was distinctly ambivalent. Everyone else who knew about this related to it out of his or her own internal agenda. Jim seemed free of this. Somehow the certainty of his own death gave him the freedom to be radically objective; thus he helped me sort my feelings and galvanize my decision-making mechanisms.

On March 6, 1976, I was elected to that bishopric; and in many ways from that moment on, both of us knew that we were dying. I was dying to my life in Richmond; he was dying to his life in this world. Certainly his was the more ultimate experience, but suddenly in a very existential way, many of his emotions and realities became real and true for me.

I would be separated forever from that community of people in which I lived and from whom I derived my strength. Every meeting with close friends was laden with the presence and the pain of that separation. I felt guilty about leaving. Some dealt with the impending separation by rejecting me "ahead of time," sometimes with overt hostility. I began to understand why it is so difficult for so many people to relate openly and honestly to a person who is dying. It is difficult to relate to any separation that hurts. I began to see as never before the guilt, the rejection, the hostility that is part of both death and bereavement. This I shared only with Jim, who could understand and interpret.

In these days he entered my life as deeply as I had entered his. We treasured the time we had together.

And we knew a level of life that I at least had never known before. I find words inadequate to describe it, but there was an intensity, a vitality, a transcendence about my relationship with Jim that was unique. In that relationship life expanded, time seemed to be a lost dimension, and God became a reality that was more than a word, more than a power. God was a kind of eternal presence that embraced us both. We explored this with the same openness with which we had explored everything else and again with no sense of embarrassment, no phoniness, no retreats into an unreal piety. We prayed together, but the quality of the life we shared with each other was holier than the words of prayer.

Jim had been relatively active in church. He had been a member of the choir. At this time he wanted to be a lay reader, and I arranged it. In that capacity he read lessons in public worship and administered the wine at Communion services. He was not always steady of either foot or voice. By this time mouth ulcers from his medication were a most unpleasant physical symptom. But he was determined to make this public witness, and he did. Privately, we would sing hymns together. He would play the piano with a lusty beat and sing at the top of his voice. In a very deliberate manner he also worked out every detail of his funeral service.

As April and May came, Jim's deterioration became more obvious. His hospital stays were longer, his days without overpowering medication were fewer. The process of separation was occurring. Our relationship began to shift. Jim felt freer to be dependent. Sometimes our visits were spent in silence. Words seemed not to matter. Sometimes his mind was affected, and he talked of fantasies and fears. At one point he became convinced that his wife, Ruth, was dying, but that soon passed.

For the last month of his life, it was as if Jim had already died. He was beyond pain, beyond most of his relationships, beyond this world. Somehow I was able to be there with him. So deeply had our lives touched the source of life in the other that we escaped most of the limitations of human existence. Jim was alive, full, free, whole even as he was dying, and I was more alive than ever before because of his gifts to me. I had long suspected that at the heart of each human life there is a vitality, a power, a quality of life that seldom emerges into our consciousness, so broken and fragmented and insecure is human life. But in this dying man, somehow by the grace of God, I had been allowed to enter that vibrant core and to share it.

What is there, I am convinced, is a transcendent presence that participates in all that we mean by the words *God* and *heaven*. One does not have to be dying to risk letting this power be known, but human beings instinctively resist the entrance of another human life into the holiest part of their being. (To share our souls might be the way traditional pious language would put it.) And because we are so afraid, we seldom really live or love or risk or dare to be. A dying man invited me beyond his security shell and allowed me to invite him beyond my security shell; and the deeper we dared to live in that relationship, the more I knew what transcendence meant, the more certain I was that God was real and that there was life beyond this life.

I think I have glimpsed it. I believe I have touched it. I am even convinced I have entered it. It is not separate from this life. It is rather the unexplored, even denied, inner core of this life. If one could be free of the brokenness of humanity, the distortions of human insecurity, then this power could be seen in that person in a startling new way. Suddenly, it dawned on me that this might be a new way to look at that life I call *Lord* and *Christ,* that being who in some way broke every human barrier, including the barrier of death.

Two or three days before my last service at St. Paul's Church, I saw Jim in the hospital for the last time. He was not conscious. I sat quietly in his room for a few minutes, then I talked to him. It was a monologue. Basically, I thanked him for his ministry to me, for allowing me to see things I had never seen before and to understand truths I had never understood before. Then I prayed, blessed him, and left.

On Sunday, May 30, 1976, I held my last Sunday service as rector of St. Paul's Church. The organist played and the choir sang as the benediction hymn the Jewish round, "Sholom Chaverim" ("Go in Peace, Dear Friend"). A chapter of my life was closing. It would never be the same.

On Tuesday, June 1, the day my resignation became effective, Jim Campbell died. We held his funeral on Thursday, June 3. It was my last official act as rector of that parish. For the benediction hymn the organist played and the choir sang "Sholom Chaverim." A chapter in his life was closing. It would never be the same.

There is something beyond time and space. There is life beyond every human limitation of life, even the limitation of death. The way one discovers that is not by escaping life, but rather by daring to live life, by scaling its heights, exploring its depths, facing its risks, penetrating its barriers. I did that with Jim Campbell;

and because I did, I will never be the same, and death will never be ultimate to me again. Finally, in my relationship with Jim Campbell I found a clue that enabled me to look again at the biblical drama of Easter and to see things I had never seen before. Suddenly all of my study and my research came together in a new way.

Chapter 3

Jesus—Tester of Barriers

Jim Campbell made me aware of how much of life lies forever dormant and unexplored in the normal course of events. When one dares to enter deeply into life's potential, one sees quickly just how little of that potential is ever realized. "In the midst of life we are in death" far more often than most of us imagine. Yet many people do seem to dream and to yearn for something more. All of the human relations experiments (group life laboratories, transactional analysis groups, marriage encounters, personal witnessing groups, communal living experiments, even some of the bizarre group sexual activities) seem to be attempts by human beings to get beneath the barriers and to explore the mystery, the meaning of life. Jesus' promise in the Fourth Gospel, "I have come that you might have life in all its fullness," is not a promise that frequently finds fulfillment in the ordinary life of the church. Indeed, not infrequently, life in the institutional church is quite closed, authoritarian, and seems organized to *control* life and feelings.

As a parish priest, I was always drawn to the "Easter Christian." I deplored the kind of judgmental and caustic remarks that so many members of my profession frequently seemed to level at these people. I remember as a seminary student attending a church in Alexandria, Virginia, on Palm Sunday and hearing the rector urge his congregation to come to the earlier Easter services on the next Sunday so that there would be enough seats at the major service "for those who want to make their semiannual peace with God." I think we fail to recognize the motivation that causes people to swell the ranks of worshipers on Easter Day.

There is, of course, the attraction of the music, the pageantry, the flowers, the spring fashions, the burst of new life in nature that exalts the human spirit. But I am convinced that the Easter worshiper is compelled to come to church for deeper reasons than any or all of these.

There is in the heart of every human being a yearning, a hope, a desire to taste life on levels that few of us achieve. It is a fearful, threatening, haunting desire. The group encounter experiments scare far more people than they attract. While most people are unwilling to risk the anxiety of personal exposure that they cannot control, they still yearn for that community where they can know and be known, love and be loved, accept and be accepted, forgive and be forgiven. To find this on any level expands life; to find it on maximum levels calls us into nothing less than a new being.

Human life is lived within all sorts of safety barriers, protective fences, and limiting forces. These barriers create our loneliness, our isolation, our fears. They enable many of us to exist without living or to content ourselves with living on the safest and most shallow of levels. The ultimate barrier of death creates the deepest fear, the deepest vulnerability; but perhaps worst of all, the presence of death lurking with its sense of inevitability on the edges of our consciousness prevents many of us from daring to live at all. Hence, the Easter story touches a very deep chord inside us, for if the ultimate barrier of death can be breached or has been breached, then perhaps there are countless levels of life that can be experienced.

So Easter appeals to hidden dreams, forlorn hopes that life is more than we experience it to be in living and that all of the barriers of life, including the final barrier of death, may be finite. There is enormous power in that possibility. This power, this yearning, this unadulterated hope is, I believe, that which fills the churches of Christendom year after year on Easter Day.

The Easter Christian comes to church on that special day. But he or she most often is not convinced, and the Sunday after Easter is still "low" Sunday. The symbols of Easter have an inexorable magnetic appeal that for at least one Sunday a year are able to set aside the doubt, the rational objections of a scientifically oriented, secularized nonbelieving society. But it does not last, and old patterns return.

I do not want to see these persons dismissed by the church, for I am convinced that the Easter Christian's inner need dwells in the life and heart of every child of the twentieth century. They are not hostile to the church or to the Easter story; rather they come on that one day more eager than they themselves seem to know. They listen to the mind-boggling claim made by the church for its Lord: the claim that death has been and therefore can be conquered; the claim that one who was dead lived again with a life that was indestructible; the claim that if we are touched by this life, we can share resurrection power; the claim that we can be set free to live in a way we have never lived before, free from fear, free from death. That is what the Easter Christian yearns to believe. There is not a life so calloused or a heart so cold that does not join in this yearning.

But no one wants to be deluded. We do not want to pretend to believe or to practice a kind of self-hypnosis. Our attitude toward the issue of life itself cannot rest on the flimsiness of our wishing that certain things were so. Yet we hope, and this hope is annually fed by the symbols and the appeal of Easter. To explore that symbol and its truth is now our task.

When relationships grow and deepen, language takes on a new and different meaning. The more open, honest, and real a relationship is, the less important the rational limits of language seem to be. I am not drawn to the charismatic phenomenon we call *glossolalia* or "speaking in tongues." Yet I can understand the black preacher who suggested that if lovers in the act of lovemaking can communicate with sounds that are nonsensical to anyone other than themselves but deeply communicative in the ecstasy of their own relationship, so a worshiper of the living God might speak to that God in a nonsensical language. Only outside the context of the ecstasy of that relationship and moment of worship would it be nonsensical.

So without being anti-intellectual, let me suggest that a rational exposition of the language of Easter might *not be* the doorway to the truth that lies under that language. I do know that the more Jim Campbell shared his life and his inner struggles with me, the less my ability to interpret or explain that life in rational words became essential to our relationship. My words also became less effective vehicles for conveying the meaning of that experience with Jim to others who did not share in it. When I began to understand that, I also began to understand something of the problem that faced the biblical writers. How can mere words give rational shape to the experience they had, an experience that broke every barrier of their previous life experience? For that was what Easter did.

If Easter is truth as I believe it is, it is truth that stretches the mind beyond the limits of finite rationality. It is the perception of a new realm breaking in, a new creation being born. It is a truth that calls us to dream, to soar, and to express our dreaming, our soaring with words that also dream and soar, with symbols that are open-ended pointers, with poetry that frees the spirit. It is this language that we confront in the biblical narratives of Easter. Listen to these symbols:

> *There was darkness over the whole land.*
> *The veil in the temple was split from top to bottom.*
> *There was an earthquake.*
> *The massive stone before the tomb was miraculously rolled away.*
> *The resurrection message was spoken by the lips of angels.*
> *Suddenly he was in the midst of them.*
> *Touch me not, for I have not yet ascended.*
> *All power is given to me in heaven and on earth.*
> *He breathed on them, and they received the Holy Spirit.*

First we must learn not to literalize the language. Rather our task is to go beneath the words and explore the power they seek to portray. We open ourselves to that power. We test it in other relationships. That is the way to explore the meaning of Easter.

Second, I would suggest that for many people in our age God is not real because they look for God in the wrong place or in an inadequate form. They are captives of their own traditions and images. Resurrection seems absurd because they conceive of it only as an event that occurs after death in what appears to be a fairyland of make-believe. These concepts have to be destroyed before the reality of God and the power of resurrection can be experienced.

The biblical God is not a kindly, comfortable father figure who lives beyond the skies and who protects, watches over, and guides our lives, eliciting from us warm, childlike feelings. The God of the Bible is creator. In his own image has he made us, to live at one with him, with each other, and with ourselves. Life in all its fullness, love with all its inclusiveness, being with all its potential are attributes of this God. The biblical narrative pictures God as a living force in history, not as a removed deity met in mystic contemplation.

The call of this God to us is a call to live, to love, to be. We do not confront or encounter this God when we retreat from life into something isolated like religion and designated by the word holy. We find God, rather, when we enter life, when we penetrate through life, when we dare to have the courage to be ourselves with another. So if God is to be found, there must be a commitment to live, to risk, to love, to be outside our self-imposed security shells. When we take this step, the meaning of resurrection begins to dawn.

Resurrection is not just something that occurs beyond time in a moment we symbolize as the mythological day of judgment, but we are resurrected into ever-expanding cycles of life every time love touches our lives, calls us out of our shells, and dares us to risk living while endowing us with the courage to be ourselves.

All of us have experienced loneliness. We also know misunderstanding, isolation, shame, fear, alienation. We know what it means to be hurt, to be rejected. When we live in these dark moments of life, we become closed, inward-directed, fortress-like. We become insensitive. We want to retaliate. Relationships are broken. Loneliness is enhanced. We cannot deliver ourselves from these emotions of hurt and fear. We can only wait and hope.

Then across the chasm of our isolation there comes the gift of love, and this love heals; it accepts, it dispels fear, it embraces with understanding. Love lifts us up and stands us on our feet. It gives us the courage to live again, to dare again, to risk loving again. That is resurrection. It is love giving life, love breaking into our loneliness. When we know love, we are lifted into life, resurrected life, life that can never be totally destroyed again.

When one has received a diagnosis of death and discovers that in the brief time left to live he or she can meet another on levels of friendship not ever before experienced, something startling occurs. One may discover that the hidden fears that have been harbored for a lifetime can be shared, and a new level and a quality of life is met that in its power destroys the fear of dying. The quality of life outweighs the quantity of life. That is what Jim Campbell taught me. To enter the depth of life, to explore the quality of life became for me the clue, the angle of vision by which the finitude of life might be viewed and the power of resurrection might be explored.

If one can find reservoirs of life and love that are

available in human relationships, it is not quite so difficult to begin to search for the source of these gifts: a source of life, a source of love, a ground of being that is eternal, unchanging, and intensely personal. Can any name other than God embrace this reality? And can any path to this God be found other than the path of discovering the power that enables the recipient to have the capacity to live, the ability to love, and the courage to be?

When one of us stands inside this experience it is not so strange or so miraculous for us to envision one life lived among us who was totally alive, completely loving, perfectly being what he was created to be. In this life, all that God is might be seen, met, engaged, revealed, experienced, worshiped. This life we call the Christ.

We examine the records we have that tell us about this Jesus. All portray a life before whom barriers fall away. His capacity to love embraced all of those whom others regarded as unlovable. His ability to live was so powerful, so complete that there was both a constant and magnetic attraction as well as a deep and sinister fear that he elicited from those who long ago traded life for security. His willingness to be all that God created him to be gave him an unearthly freedom from needs, either physical or those of status. His security of being was so deep that he could give himself away totally, completely.

If God is the source of life, love, and being, then to meet the fullness of life, the completeness of love, the totality of being in a human life is to meet God. In his life the fullness of humanity was also seen. In the narratives of Holy Scripture, we watch that life as it prepares to confront the ultimate barrier of death. Perhaps life is more than any of us has dreamed, we say.

Perhaps there are untold riches to life that we could explore, but no matter how high we fly, there still seems to be the ultimate barrier of finitude, the last enemy called death against which we collide and finally lose. Can we experience a reality that will break that barrier? Could the completely alive Jesus?

His capacity to love revealed that he had received an infinite amount of love. His ability to be open appeared to be uncompromised by religious, national, or racial exclusion. His ability to restore that which was broken or distorted to the wholeness God intended inspired all sorts of miraculous stories about him. He lived out a freedom and a personal wholeness that was both powerfully attractive and deeply threatening. This threat led his enemies finally to nail him to a cross. He was executed.

But even as his life was being destroyed, from him there continued to flow a love that embraced those who wielded the power of death. As he died, he was far more alive than those who were still to live a few years longer. In the moments between Good Friday and Easter, this life seemed to test that ultimate barrier of death, and somehow people were convinced that Jesus prevailed. He was known to them not as a fading memory, but as an *Eternal Now*.[3] He was to them not a subjective presence but a generating power.

In age after age, other lives have been convinced that they have met this power afresh. They have been set free to live by this power. They have begun to press the limits of their potential because of this power. They have become real persons, selves they never dreamed they could be. They have been willing to risk and meet and know and love in a way that called them again and again into a resurrected life.

It is because of these experiences that Christians can and do dare to suggest that the barrier to life we call death is not an ultimate barrier at all. If this barrier has been tested and broken by the fully alive Christ, then in him and through him we can touch that which is eternal and share in it. If in life we find many moments of resurrection, it is not quite so difficult to imagine or to believe that there is one ultimate resurrection and that in Jesus the Christ that resurrection has dawned and our hope of sharing in it is not a fantasy.

We are born to live, not to die, and in Christ we are restored to our own truest, deepest destiny. We share in eternity and in an ever-expanding life both here and hereafter.

Part II

The Effects
of the Easter Moment

Chapter 4

Introduction

The dynamic, energized birth of the Christian Church took place at the Moment of Easter. It had enormous power. It affected human life and human history. Before we attempt to penetrate the Moment of Easter, we must first observe, measure, and deal with the effects of Easter. Scholars may well question the objectivity and the historicity of Jesus' resurrection, but no one can doubt for a moment that something happened, the effects of which are visible, measurable, demonstrable. The Moment of Easter may have been beyond history, but its impact was not.

In this section I will attempt to lay that impact before my readers. It is an accumulation of data that I believe Christians tend to minimize. It is impressive, overwhelming evidence that needs to be spelled out and viewed in its totality. It points to the need for an explanation. It may not prove that resurrection happened, but it certainly does prove that something happened—something of significance, power, and impressive strength. The issue is so personal, so immense, so life-determining that even the most skeptical nonbeliever must give it consideration.

Effects cannot guarantee the full disclosure of the cause, but they can point to the reality of a cause. This process is considered legitimate in other areas of the human exploration into truth. Its use cannot be denied an opportunity to bring light to so central a moment of human history as Easter historically has been. Deductive reasoning shall be our tool in this section. The reader must make sure that he or she faces the limitations of this tool and understands what it cannot do. Only then will deductive reasoning be useful for what it can do.

When I was a child reading comic books, two advertisements were regular features in the chronicles of my favorite comic heroes. One was for the Charles Atlas Body Building Course, and the other was for a diet aid. Both featured dramatic pictorial evidence of before and after. In the Charles Atlas ad, a beach bully was always kicking sand into the eyes of a scrawny man who was too intimidated to protest. His manhood threatened by his ineptitude in front of his girl friend, he simply seethed and yearned for vindication. Cutting out an ad similar to the one on that page, this scrawny victim of oppression sent for the Charles Atlas Body Building Course. It arrived, and in due time he was a veritable Mr. America with bulging biceps. The final picture in the advertisement took us back to the beach sometime later. Again the bully kicked sand, but this time the muscled graduate of the Charles Atlas School belted him and ran him off the beach. Vindicated, he embraced his proud girl friend and gave thanks to the source of his newfound strength and invited his readers to follow his example and enroll at once so they too would no longer be pushed around.

In the reducing plan featuring a diet aid, the first picture was of an enormous woman in a ridiculous-looking bathing suit. The fat descended her legs in ripples that looked like high tide at Lake Tahoe, Nevada. Her face and her body were not separated by a neck. The ad suggested that this was a photograph of Mrs. Jane Doe before she started using this diet aid. The second picture was of a svelte, trim woman with dimensions that sound like those of a beauty pageant contestant. She testified to the effectiveness of the product, citing the change in her dress size, in her husband's attitude, and in her joy in life. She too urged the overweight reader to act at once by sending in the attached coupon.

Both of these ads were using deductive reasoning. They showed the person before using the product and then afterwards. There was a discernible, measurable change. Obviously, something had happened. They suggested that their explanation accounted for the change. The ads were effective only to the degree that the reader believed their explanations. That the advertised product produced the pictured results cannot be proved by this process. That something happened if the photographs honestly reveal the same person at two different times in the same life is indisputable. In some sense this process is like observing the wind. You can see signs of its presence, you can feel its cooling or warming breath, you can measure its impact, but the wind itself cannot be seen.

It is important that we understand the effects of the Easter Moment. We will look at people and traditions before Easter and these same people and traditions after Easter. Incredible changes will be obvious. One cannot prove in this manner that the Resurrection of Jesus happened, but one can prove that something happened—something big and powerful, for it left an enormous impact upon the life and history of the world. To use a double negative, the Easter Moment cannot be nothing. It has to be something.

I would like to think of this section as a trial, an attempt to gather evidence to cause a jury to reach a verdict. So think of the following chapters as witnesses telling their story on the witness stand, trying to demonstrate that something happened at the Moment of Easter. If you as the jury decide they have made their case, perhaps you will read on.

Chapter 5

Peter—A Changed Man

I call to the witness stand Simon, son of Jonah, known as Peter.

One of the most human, lovable, and significant figures to emerge from the Gospel narratives is the man we call Simon Peter. Peter was his nickname. In Greek it meant rock. It might not be different from the nickname "Rocky" that has come to mean a tough fellow. It is a favorite nickname in the boxing world. Two of the greats of fisticuff history, Rocky Graziano, the former middleweight champion whose three fights with Tony Zale made boxing history, and Rocky Marciano, the only undefeated heavyweight champion of the world, both found in the name Rocky a special identification.

Nicknames are our attempt to identify people by some special characteristic. Peter the Rock was tough, aggressive, loud, bombastic. He was a ne'er-do-well fisherman who always wanted to be someone important. But he was caught on a kind of inescapable wheel of fortune. There was no great wealth for people in the fishing trade in the first century in Galilee, Peter's home. The fisherman lived from day to day, from catch to catch. It was hard to get ahead. Peter lived with his mother-in-law. In Jewish society of the first century that was not done unless economic circumstances required it. Interestingly, the Bible never mentions his wife, but a man can hardly have a mother-in-law without having a wife, so her existence is assumed.

There are two versions of how Peter's life became associated with Jesus of Nazareth. Matthew, Mark, and Luke, the synoptic gospels, say Jesus called him directly from his fishing trade into discipleship. The Fourth Gospel says that Andrew, his brother, after meeting and staying with Jesus, came and took Peter to the one he believed to be the Messiah. Whatever the history was of that meeting, there was no doubt that it was the significant and determinative confrontation in the life of Simon Peter.

If the New Testament account is historically accurate, Peter and the other disciples were associated with Jesus in some way prior to the time they were invited into the special status of the twelve. As *followers,* they had a chance to observe without commitment, to feel the power of this Jesus, to be affected by his life. No relationship develops instantaneously. No one reveals his inner core to another until such time as the kind of trust has developed that guarantees the gentle and loving acceptance of that revelation. So it was with Peter, and the Gospel narratives record in the bluntest and least favorable fashion possible the struggle Peter had in this growing relationship. The needs of his ego always seemed to outstep his ability. He covered his insecurity with aggressive behavior and incessant bragging.

I suspect that when Jesus invited Peter and the others to the special status of discipleship the old fisherman's heart swelled with a certain amount of pride. Perhaps this meant he was important, *a somebody,* he thought; and this man seemed to need to be *a somebody* more than most. The picture the New Testament paints of him is that of a deeply insecure man who in an almost childlike way craved recognition and basked in the sunshine of attention. To cover this part of his personality, he developed a dominating external style. It worked so long as no one got too near or looked too closely.

As with every human community, the disciple band had to grow together. They had to establish relationships, rank, and priority—even a pecking order. Peter's aggressive and loud manner quickly identified him, if not as the leader, at least as a power with which the others had to reckon. Peter was always the first to speak. He assumed the position of honor. When Jesus asked the disciples in general a question, Peter in particular gave the answer. He did not pause or inquire if there might be other possibilities. It was as if he were saying, "I have spoken; there is therefore nothing else to say."

At the town of Caesarea Philippi in the northern Jordan River valley Jesus had a remarkable conversation with his disciples, the Gospel of Mark tells us. "Who do people say that I am?" he asked. There was a bit of brainstorming, and the answers flowed without comment. "Jeremiah." "John the Baptist, one of the old prophets." These were among the answers. But then Jesus turned the conversation sharply to confront an important and existential issue. "But who do you say that I am?" he asked. Peter instinctively and impulsively blurted out more than subsequent conversation revealed that he understood, "You are the Christ, the Son of the Living God." Perhaps surprised, Jesus acknowledged the answer and even praised Peter for his insight and then began to talk about what it meant to be the Christ, the Son of the Living God. "It does not mean success or glory. It may mean defeat and failure. It may be a faithfulness that will endure suffering and death before the messianic purpose can be accomplished."

This was too much for Peter, who interrupted and in effect demanded that Jesus be the kind of Christ Peter needed him to be. This won for Peter the New Testament's sharpest rebuke, "Get thee behind me, Satan." Peter was embarrassed but not defeated. Subsequent events reveal he was not changed.

Peter's aggressive way did win for him a position in the inner corps of advisors; Peter, James, and John emerge in the Gospel narrative as the leaders of the band, the trusted ones who were allowed to share the more intimate moments of Jesus' life. Whatever the experience was that we call the transfiguration, one thing is certain: Peter was involved in that moment. The details are shrouded in mystery, but Mark in particular goes out of his way to indicate that Peter's role was cumbersome, oafish, and without the slightest bit of understanding. The details as Mark gives them are these:

Jesus chose his inner corps to go up a mountain with him to pray. While he was there, his raiment became lustrous, brilliant, perfectly white. In this transfigured state, the father of Jewish law, Moses, and the father of the prophetic movement, Elijah, suddenly appeared to him and talked with him. How Peter recognized Moses and Elijah we are not told, but there was no doubt expressed about their identification. Peter must have been beside himself with pride. There he was with the heroes of the Jewish heritage, talking to the one who invited him into discipleship.

More and more Peter must have been intrigued that Jesus chose twelve. That was the number of the tribes of Israel. One of the messianic symbols was the establishment of the new Israel, and Peter began to have delusions of the greatness that was in store for him. So even in this strange setting of the transfiguration, Peter blurted out with his limited but egocentric understanding, "Lord, it is good to be here. Let us erect three tabernacles to mark this occasion. One for Moses, one for Elijah, and one for you, Jesus." Perhaps Peter hoped that somewhere on that monument it might also humbly mention that "Peter was here." At the very least he could tell people about it and show them the monument for which he had been responsible. At that moment, Mark says, a cloud overshadowed them, and a voice spoke out of the cloud, and Peter was rebuked. Mark apologizes for Peter, remarking, "He did not know what he was saying." The voice affirmed Jesus as unique, special, not to be confused with prophets of a lower order like Moses or Elijah. Peter could not see beyond his own needs; and the less he saw, the louder and more aggressive he became.

The pattern is quite consistent in the biblical story. We see it next in the story of the Last Supper. The more Jesus discussed the impending passion, the less Peter either understood or was enthralled. Loudly he protested his loyalty, his willingness to defend his master. Finally, Jesus said, "Peter, even you will deny me before the cock crows," a reference probably to a shift in the guard rather than to the crowing of a rooster.[4] At this public suggestion that Peter might not be the strong man he pretended to be, Peter became indignant. "Even if every one of these people forsake you, I will be faithful," he swore with his voice rising several decibels. It is always so with those who cower in fear behind the facade of bravado.

People who have to dominate are never strong people. We dominate to cover our fear, our insecurity, to prevent our weakness from being discovered. Parents who have to control their children, presidents who cannot tolerate a hint of disloyalty in their cabinets, bishops who cannot hear or allow dissent in the clergy, bosses who have to regulate every moment of their employees' time, husbands who cannot allow their wives to become competent and individual persons with lives of their own—these display symptoms of weakness, not of strength. The sign of weakness is to rage and shout whenever the strong image of domination is called into question and the facade of caring or benevolent paternalism or control is threatened with exposure. This was Peter.

When one brags too loudly or too publicly, the ensuing disintegration is impossible to hide. This is what seems to have happened to Peter. The day we call Maundy Thursday concluded, according to the Fourth Gospel, with Jesus taking a basin and a towel and proceeding to wash the disciples' feet. Peter watched in increasing apprehension as Jesus neared him. Those who are bossy, pretending to be great, cannot stand it when one whom even they recognize as greater acts toward them with humble acquiescence. So when Jesus knelt to do the servant's task to the mighty Peter, Peter backed up declaring, "You'll never wash my feet!" To this Jesus replied, "Peter, if I do not wash your feet, you have no part in me." Peter, trapped in his own mock humility, tried to recoup his losses. "Then Lord," he responded, "wash all of me."

Following that supper, the passion narrative moves to the Garden of Gethsemane where the evangelists assert that Peter once more failed to cover himself with glory. Jesus took Peter, James, and John with him to that garden and asked them to stand watch while he prayed. He left them and went a short distance in what was an intensely personal moment of final decision-making, so intense that Luke suggests that Jesus' sweat was like great drops of blood. That is doubtless a bit of writer's license, but it captures the mood of that moment in Jesus' life. Returning to Peter and the disciples, he found them sleeping, hardly a flattering picture. A second and third time the scene was repeated. The disappointing question, "Could you not watch with me one brief hour," was asked but never answered.

Then Judas and the temple guard appeared. The kiss was offered; the arrest was made. The disciples fled. The only attempt to whitewash Peter is in the Johannine narrative where it is suggested that Peter drew his sword and cut off the ear of the servant of the high priest. Even in this account (which no New Testament scholar I know of treats as history), however, Jesus once again rebuked Peter. "It is not your sword but your faithfulness I need, Peter, and you obviously do not yet understand."

The Gospels do tell us that after fleeing, Peter alone of the twelve returned to watch the proceedings. Perhaps he sought a chance to help, perhaps he just wanted to make good his boast, but we see him next in the courtyard of the high priest, alone and vulnerable. Here a great personal drama was acted out.

Without Jesus, Peter once again was a nobody. No one deferred to him or listened to him. Those aching insecurities he tried so hard to keep hidden now rushed out of him. He tried to act *Rocky*. It fooled no one. It is not an insignificant detail of the story that the rout of Peter was at the hands of the lowest member of the social caste, a domestic slave girl.

It is always the mob spirit to side with the one who is perceived as victorious. When an arrest was made, the crowd assumed that guilt was both pronounced and deserved. It was not long before guilt by association was practiced. Jesus was clearly the victim, and those in the courtyard were observing all of the rules of the game.

The servant girl confronted Peter, and much to his dismay she announced, "This man is a follower of the condemned man." In one stroke Peter's dignity was affronted, and his cover was removed. He was not used to being addressed in so flippant and hostile a manner by one who was clearly his social inferior. And immediately and instinctively he responded out of his need for self-preservation. "I do not know what you're talking about," he snapped, trying to avoid the issue and not perjure himself at the same time. He moved to slip out of the courtyard, only to discover that the servant girl followed him repeating the charge. "This is a follower of the condemned man." Peter was seething. "Oh wretched, damnable, nosey, talkative woman," he probably thought even as he uttered an oath and shouted, "I am not." Weak people frequently resort to oaths when they fear that their lies are not being believed. Somehow to swear and shout is supposed to make one more believable. It does not.

Outside, others picked up the slave girl's charge. "Why, you are one of his followers," they asserted. "You dress like a Galilean, your speech has a Galilean accent." Peter was trapped, and the vise was closing tighter and tighter. He looked from person to person, seeking some glimmer of support. There was none. Then the ultimate denial flowed out of his lips, "I do not know the man of whom you speak." I do not know the one I have followed for all this time, shared life with in community, listened to him speak, watched him heal, pledged to him my loyalty. I do not even know the man I wanted to memorialize with the greatest heroes of Israel. This was Peter on the night of the arrest, broken, weak, and, worst of all, publicly revealed. One Gospel says Jesus turned and looked at Peter. Whether he did or did not is insignificant, for the pain of being caught between the person he wanted to be and the person he saw himself to be at that moment was more than Peter could stand. He wept like a baby, his bravado now disintegrated. The strong man who wanted to be somebody, who cultivated the image of dominance, now stood before them, undressed as it were, a nobody, routed by a slave girl, and weakling he had always been. It is a devastating portrait.

That was Peter before the Easter Moment. I see no reason to doubt the accuracy of the main lines of this biblical portrait. Perhaps some of the details could not stand the scrutiny of biblical scholarship, but there is no motive I can imagine in the early Christian writers that would cause them to create this devastating portrait of one whom they regarded as a hero. If the record were going to be doctored, it would seem far more likely for it to be doctored in a favorable manner. There is a strong historicity in this portrait. Peter before the Easter Moment was a Peter of weakness, failure, denial. More than that, it was probably Peter himself who made sure that this part of himself was never forgotten.

But something happened to Peter. Something so big, so powerful that his life totally turned around. His personality was reoriented. His needs for power, status, and pretending disappeared. Something ignited the potential that was in Peter and exploded him into a new life, a new being. The Peter we meet after Easter had great humility. He had a quality of fearlessness that was unbelievable. And he had a sureness so deep that he could lay his security-giving prejudices aside. Recall it was Peter, according to the book of Acts, who led the Christian Church out of the narrow boundaries of Judaism and into the Gentile mission. Peter had a dream in which a sheet was let down from heaven with animals on it that Peter had been taught were unclean. A voice from heaven invited Peter to rise, kill, and eat the forbidden animals. Peter demurred, saying he could not eat such food. The voice said, "Peter, what I have created don't you call unclean." Following this dream Peter is quoted as saying, "I now realize that God treats all people alike, no matter what race they belong to."

Finally, there is no reason to doubt the tradition of the martyrdom of Peter. How he was martyred may have been subject to some heightening or exaggeration, but the fact remains that the new Peter never again denied his Lord and went to his death willingly in witness to that Lord. No one who had read only the pre-Easter portrait of Peter in the New Testament would have imagined a brave martyrdom for him.

Peter was changed dramatically, significantly, totally. Peter before Easter and Peter after Easter are discernibly different people. Clearly, something happened to Peter. Something brought about the change. Something touched the deepest recesses of Peter's life and called forth a new being. That something was involved in whatever the Easter Moment was.

Look at Peter. Look at the witness of his life, his change. Let the power of that transformation be embraced before you dismiss Peter from the stand and prepare to call the next witness.

Chapter 6

The Disciples—
Cowards into Heroes

I call the other disciples now to come to the stand. We will seek their testimony.

The New Testament seems to be clear on the point that Jesus chose twelve men to be related to him in a special way as disciples. That, however, is as far as the certainty goes. Who constituted the twelve cannot be accurately determined. Matthew agrees with Mark in including Simon Peter; James and John, the sons of Zebedee; Andrew; Philip; Bartholomew; Matthew; Thomas; James, the son of Alphaeus; Thaddaeus; Simon the Zealot; and Judas Iscariot. Luke, however, drops Thaddaeus from his list and adds Judas, the son of James, instead. The Fourth Gospel never lists the twelve all together but talks about Nathanael's being one of the disciples. Clearly, there was confusion in the early church as to who the original twelve were. The number twelve, however, was very important symbolically. The new Israel must, like the old Israel, have twelve tribes. One of the first acts of the post-resurrection community, according to the book of Acts, was to elect Matthias to take the place of Judas Iscariot to preserve the number twelve.

Beyond this, we have only hints about the character or biography of these disciples. By and large, they appear in the biblical record to be anything but giants. They are portrayed by the Gospels very unfavorably, lacking in dignity, in understanding, and in sensitivity. None of them appears to come from the upper classes of Jewish society. Four of them (Peter, James, John, and Andrew) are identified vocationally as fishermen. Matthew seems to have been a tax collector, and Simon in one tradition is called the zealot or the patriot, which may identify him as a member of a Jewish guerilla fighting group. In another tradition he is called the Canaanean, which could indicate that he was not Jewish by blood. None of the others are identified vocationally or professionally. In the book of Acts, Matthias and Joseph, called both Barsabbas and Justus, are nominated to take Judas' position. Neither of the nominees is mentioned in any Gospel record. Barnabas and Silas also loom large in the history of the early church, but once again neither is mentioned in the Gospels.

It is certain that fishermen were probably not very high on the social scale of Judea or Galilee. And a tax collector in those days was even something of a traitor since he was a Jew willing to extort money from his fellow Jews in the service of the conquering Roman Empire. A Roman tax collector made his salary by collecting as much as he could beyond the amount set for the state by the Roman authorities. Rome allowed its tax collectors to keep for themselves all the money they could collect beyond their quotas. It was a system guaranteed to destroy trust and to build hatred. A zealot was most probably an outlaw from justice for whom both murder and robbery would be commonplace.

Other biographical notes are few and far between. James and John, the sons of Zebedee, are given the nickname *Boanerges,* (Mk. 3:17) which we are told means sons of thunder and may have been a witness to their hot tempers. A hint of this may be seen in Luke's story (Lk. 9:51ff.) about the Samaritan village that refused to receive Jesus. James and John suggested that fire be called down from heaven to consume them. It was hardly a Gospel response, and it received a rebuke from Jesus. Later James and John entered a scheme to seek to enhance their power (Mk. 10:37). Secretly they came to Jesus and requested the privilege of sitting on his right hand and on his left hand when he established his kingdom. This request, which would not be unlike a request to be assigned the positions of Secretary of State and Secretary of Defense in a new American Cabinet, was declined by Jesus ("It is not mine to give"), but it roused a considerable amount of hostility among the others who recognized that the elevation they sought would be at the expense of the other disciples.

Thomas has the nickname *The Twin,* (Jn. 11:16) but what it refers to (beyond its literal meaning) cannot be determined. The characterization of doubt is a Johannine story alone and may or may not have been an actual historical biographical note. Nathanael has also been stamped by the Johannine pen as skeptical, but somehow that was never caught up by tradition. When Nathanael was told by Philip that they had found the Messiah, identifying him as "Jesus, the son of Joseph, from Nazareth" (Jn. 1:45ff.), Nathanael snapped, "Can anything good come out of Nazareth?"

Andrew, Simon Peter's brother, emerges out of the Johannine narrative as a sensitive, self-effacing disciple. He appears to be an ordinary follower, willing to do simple and humble tasks. When called into discipleship, he first went to find his brother Peter to share the news with him and to enable Peter to enter the service of Jesus in a way clearly more significant and central than the role he, Andrew, was to play (Jn. 1:41). Indeed, Andrew's primary identity in the New Testament was that he is Simon Peter's brother, a status that he did not appear to resent. It was Andrew, the Fourth Gospel says (Jn. 6:8), who brought to Jesus the news that one lad had five barley loaves and two small fish—this in the face of a crowd numbering more than 5,000 in the wilderness, far from home and far from food. To most people that information would have been too insignificant to mention, but to Andrew no gift appeared too small to be received. John portrays Jesus as using that gift to feed the multitude. Finally, in the Fourth Gospel, some Greek citizens came to one or another of the disciples saying, "Sir, we would see Jesus," and once again Andrew appears in the humble role as guide, leading them to Jesus (Jn. 12:22).

The Fourth Gospel also portrays in a very favorable light a person identified only as the beloved disciple. Who he is scholars have never been able to determine, though his historic identification with John Zebedee is universally doubted. But in the Fourth Gospel he is portrayed as leaning on the breast of Jesus at the Last Supper (Jn. 13:23), as having Jesus assign to him from the cross the care of his mother (Jn. 19:26), and, finally, as accompanying Peter to the empty tomb and being the first to read resurrection into that scene (Jn 20:8).

In the synoptics there seems to be a triumvirate, or an inner three, that rose to become the core or leadership group (Mt. 17:1, Mk. 5:37, Lk. 8:51). They are Peter, James, and John. The fact that these three seemed to occupy leadership positions in the early church according to the book of Acts may either be read back so that they emerged as leaders of the disciple band during Jesus' life, or their leadership during Jesus' life may have established them as leaders in the early church. James Zebedee, Acts tells us, was the first of the twelve to die the death of the martyr (Acts 12:1ff.), and Peter and John were clearly the leaders of the early church until James, the Lord's brother, and Paul emerged later in the story. In any event, the triumvirate of Peter, James, and John shared with Jesus certain very special moments, such as the vision on the mount of transfiguration and the agony of the Garden of Gethsemane.

There is a hint, perhaps more than a hint, that on the level of ability alone Judas Iscariot may have been the most able one of the twelve, for he was chosen by the disciple band to handle their business affairs. He kept the money bag and was their treasurer. Scholars are uncertain as to the meaning of Iscariot. Some seem to think it relates to a Judean village named Kerioth and that originally it was Judas of Kerioth. If that is so, it makes Judas the only Judean among a disciple band of Galileans. That may offer some slight clue to his motive for betrayal. Some have suggested that when Judas realized that Jesus had no nationalistic messianic expectations and that his conflict was with the religious hierarchy and not with Rome, then the act of betrayal became his only escape. If Jesus was executed, as Judas seemed to feel he would be, then Judas as a Judean would be a marked man in a way the Galilean disciples would not be, for he would have to live his life in Judea in the shadow of those who had executed Jesus, and he would never have the anonymity that Galilee would provide the others. That, however, is all speculation based on one view of the meaning of Iscariot.

Hans Küng in his monumental book *On Being a Christian* (p. 329) suggests that Iscariot is a mutilated form of the Latin *sicarius,* which means dagger man or assassin and was a title of derision added after Good Friday. He further suggests that Judas, impelled by zealot enthusiasm, was disappointed and made contact with Jesus' enemies in order to force him to act. But this too Kung admits is pure speculation.

There are two versions of Judas' death in the Gospels. Matthew indicates (Mt. 27:3ff.) that Judas repented and tried to return the betrayal money. This was refused, and Judas went and hanged himself before the trial of Jesus was complete. Luke in the book of Acts (Acts 1:18, 19) says that Judas took the money and bought a field where he fell to his death; he burst open and all his insides spilled out, causing the people of Jerusalem to call that field *a field of blood.*

Aside from these few biographical details, the disciples are generally treated as a group, and a not too impressive group at that. They bickered constantly. They seemed to be intent on jockeying for position. Their scheming quality caused Jesus to set a child in their midst and say, "Except ye be converted, and become as little children, ye shall not enter into the kingdom of God" (Mt. 18:2). The same problem is reiterated in John's version of the time Jesus washed their feet (Jn. 13:1ff.). Over and over again he called them to the humility of love and servanthood. Time and again the disciples yearned for status and power.

When the crowd brought little children to Jesus, the disciples rebuked them, and Jesus rebuked the disciples. "Allow the little children to come to me. Do not forbid them, for such is the kingdom of God" (Mk. 10:14). The disciples seemed to be jealous when someone who was not a member of their group was healing in Jesus' name. They ordered him to stop (Mk. 9:38ff.), and once more they were rebuked by Jesus. Following the transfiguration story, the disciples are portrayed as impotent in the presence of the epileptic boy (Mk. 9:14ff.), and Jesus said to them, "How unbelieving you are. How long must I stay with you? How long do I have to put up with you?"

Time after time Jesus appears thwarted and frustrated by his disciples. They appear to lack sensitivity, insight, humility, understanding. Constantly he looked to them for response. He seldom found it. They judged by different standards. They seemed appalled when Jesus sent the rich young ruler away sorrowing (Mk. 10:22). When they listened to Jesus teaching about wealth, they responded incredulously, "Who then can be saved?" (Lk. 18:24ff.). Even in his moment of deepest agony in the Garden of Gethsemane, they were unable to watch with him for one hour. He returned to find them sleeping. When the traitor appeared, it is clear that one of the twelve upon whom he was depending had fallen. When Peter denied him, the second hope died. When he was arrested, all forsook him and fled, and the disciple band was, in effect, wiped out. Not one of the disciples is portrayed as viewing the crucifixion save for that enigmatic figure the Fourth Gospel calls the beloved disciple. No one of the disciples tended to the burial of their master. That was left most probably to the Sanhedrin.

Where did they flee? Of that we cannot be certain. Mark and Matthew seem to indicate that they fled to Galilee. Luke and John indicate that they went into hiding in Jerusalem. The twenty-first chapter of John portrays them as back in Galilee. There is agreement only that they fled, scattered and fearful. Even the ones who are purported to have stayed in Jerusalem are pictured as frightened cowards, hiding out for their lives in a well-secured, locked, and barred upper room. Both traditions probably have truth in them, but more will be said about that later. Peter and one or two others may have stayed in hiding in Jerusalem. The others may have fled to Galilee. But in either case it was not a performance to be admired. They were scared, they were cowardly, they were disillusioned, they were scattered, and they were despairing.

Once again, it is difficult to suggest that this clear portrait of the behavior of the disciples is not accurate. It is customary not to allow all of the warts to show in the rendering of history. The tendency is to whitewash leaders, to clean up faults, to repair images. When the Gospels were written, the twelve were held in high esteem. The motive for portraying them as ungainly cowards would be minimal. But the record is so clear. Before the Easter Moment there was little reason to hope for much from the group known as the twelve. Their behavior was scandalous. But something happened.

The Moment of Easter dawned for this motley group. They were reconstituted by that experience. They emerged out of hiding. They were galvanized into action. They were energized by some enormous force. They left their sanctuaries. They lost their cowardly fear. Nothing ever frightened them again. They returned to Jerusalem. They took to the streets. They proclaimed their story. "Jesus lives!" "Death cannot contain him!" They took on the world. They prevailed. They endured ridicule, arrest, torture, beatings, and even death. But they never deviated from their story. They never wavered. Cowards were turned into heroes. Men in hiding for fear became fearless martyrs. Death frightened them no more. It held no further power over them. Why should they fear those who could only hurt or kill their bodies?

They launched a mission and a movement that literally exploded onto the stage of human history. It created a new holy day. It broke out of the limitation of Jewish nationalism into a universalism. It conquered the civilized Western world in less than 300 years. At the very heart of that movement was an unshakable conviction and an unwavering confidence that life, not death, was the final destiny for the human being and that this destiny had been experienced in the life of Jesus of Nazareth. Something happened in the Moment of Easter that created enormous changes and ignited enormous power.

The witness of the disciples is before you. Weigh it well before you dismiss them from the stand.

Chapter 7

James — From Critical Sibling to Ardent Worshiper

I call James, the brother of Jesus, known as James the Just, to the stand.

There are three men named James in the early history of the Christian Church. Inevitably, there is confusion among them. One is James, the son of Zebedee, the brother of John, nicknamed Boanerges by Jesus. He is a major figure in the Gospels, one of the inner circle of three. But according to the book of Acts, he was put to death by Herod Agrippa, grandson of Herod the Great, sometime around the year A.D. 44. He was the first member of the twelve to be martyred.

The second James was the son of Alphaeus. He may or may not have had a mother named Mary who came to the tomb at dawn on the first day of the week according to Mark, Luke, and possibly Matthew. It is hard to imagine that there is a fourth James or that James Zebedee's mother is the Mary intended. James, the son of Alphaeus, is sometimes known as James the

Less. Other than a listing in Matthew, Mark, Luke, and Acts as one of the original twelve disciples, this James fades from the biblical record and is heard of no more.

The third James is a figure that looms larger and larger in the Christian story and, in fact, becomes so well known that a reference to him is actually made in the writings of the Jewish historian Flavius Josephus in A.D. 90. He appears to have been murdered by a mob in Jerusalem around the year A.D. 62 and to have acquired the nickname James the Just. Josephus makes reference to this (*Antiquities* 20–9 N 1) calling him "James, the brother of Jesus, the so-called Christ." It is clear that he exercised great power in the early church. It is also obvious that he was the brother of Jesus of Nazareth.

The idea that Jesus had other brothers and sisters is very overtly stated on at least two occasions in the Gospels and more often than that in both Galatians and Acts. That never bothered the early church or the biblical writers. However, as Christianity moved out of its Jewish womb and into the Mediterranean world, its content began to be shaped by a Neoplatonic world view, which was basically dualistic. Reality was divided into two realms: one contained things spiritual and the other things physical. Good was identified with the realm of the spirit and evil with the realm of the physical. God was spiritual; the world was physical. The biblical concept of creation clearly faded. Suddenly in that world indulging the appetites of the body came to be considered evil. In classical ascetical theology the body was meant to be mortified by the Christian, not indulged. So celibacy was a higher vocation than marriage. Virginity was a higher calling than motherhood.

Before the second century passed, the ideal woman was not just the Virgin Mary, but the perpetually virgin Mary. Before the process was concluded, she had been immaculately conceived (1854) and bodily assumed (1950). Sex could not be part of the image of the Virgin Mary. It is interesting to note that one of the earliest biblical references to the birth of Jesus is written by Paul in Romans (A.D. 58) where he assumes the birth was normal and human. He writes (Rom. 1:2–4), "As to his humanity, he was born a descendant of David. As to his divine holiness, he was shown with great power to be the Son of God by being raised from the dead." In later Christian thought, Mary became Queen of Heaven, the Bride of Christ, and even coredeemer. Interestingly enough, one bodily and sexual function was left to Mary in the devotional literature of the medieval church. She could nurse. And the Holy Mother's breast milk was given credit for miraculous cures.[5] The production of Mother Mary's milk was, however, separated from any other part of her sexuality. Any tradition that regarded sex as defilement, that went to such lengths as immaculate conception to deliver Mary from any taint of sexuality, that declared her perpetually virgin must in fact edit or even attempt to rewrite or reunderstand the Bible. That was certainly done in Christian history. The brothers of Jesus became cousins, and the confusion of James, the son of Alphaeus, with James, the Lord's brother, was a helpful tool in preserving Mary's virginity.

Even the birth narrative of Matthew obviously did not intend to declare Mary perpetually virgin. That author says Joseph, learning of the child's divine origin in a dream, married Mary (Mt. 2:24,25). "But he had no sexual relations with her *before* she gave birth to a son." Clearly for Matthew after the birth of Jesus, Joseph and Mary lived out a normal family pattern.

With mild redactions by both Matthew and Luke that are not substantive, Mark's account of the visit of Jesus' mother and his brothers to him during the early part of his Galilean ministry finds inclusion in each of the three synoptic Gospels. Jesus had created quite a stir. People were talking. Not all of the talk seems to have been flattering. Jesus returned to his home in Nazareth to teach. The crowd was so intense that Jesus and his disciples had no time to eat. His family heard about this, says Mark, and "set out to get him, because people were saying he has gone mad" (Mk. 3:20ff.). Some teachers of the law were claiming he was demon-possessed. "He has Beelzebub in him. The chief of the demons gives him power to drive other demons out." Jesus countered this, according to Mark, with such sayings as "How can Satan cast out Satan? A house divided against itself cannot stand." He goes on to allude to the unforgivable sin of being a person who says evil things about the Holy Spirit, which Mark explains he said because someone accused him of being possessed by an evil spirit (Mk. 3:29).

Then Jesus' mother and brothers arrived. (Since Joseph never appears after the birth stories, there is a presumption that he had by this time died.) They could not get into the house because of the crowd, so they sent a message to him. The crowd told Jesus that his mother and brothers were asking for him. Jesus declined to go, saying rather that his true mother and sisters and brothers are those who obey God's will. Clearly there was no trust, no understanding that flowed between Jesus and his primary physical family.

Only the note that his family came because they thought he might be mad is deleted by both Matthew and Luke. It is easy to understand why.

Later in the Gospel of Mark (Mk. 6:1–6) and substantially copied in Matthew (13:53–58), another episode involving Jesus' family is related. Jesus was teaching in the Nazareth synagogue. When the people heard him, they were amazed. "Where did he get this wisdom?" they inquired. "Isn't he the carpenter, the son of Mary and the brother of James, Joses, Judah, and Simon? Are not his sisters living here? And so they rejected him." This was the episode that caused Jesus to say, "A prophet is not without honor anywhere except in his own home, by his relatives and his family." Luke changes this story dramatically, leaving the Markan text almost completely. He substitutes the question "Is not this Joseph's son?" (Lk. 4:22) and omits all other family references. However, this passage once again reveals that the relationships of understanding between Jesus and his family were not very cordial.

There are two references in the Fourth Gospel that bear comment. In the bread passages of John (6:41ff.,) the Jews are portrayed as grumbling about him because he had said such things as, "I am the bread that came down from heaven." So they said, "This man is Jesus, the son of Joseph, isn't he? We know his father and his mother. How then does he now say he came down from heaven?" It is interesting to note that there is no birth narrative in the Fourth Gospel. No virgin birth story is told by this evangelist. And if, as seems to be the case, John is the last Gospel to be written, his deliberate omission of a miraculous birth story after both Matthew and Luke have included it is telling. Of course, neither Mark, the first Gospel to be written, nor Paul, who wrote all of his epistles before the first Gospel appeared, ever mentions a birth tradition.

To follow this thread still further, in the Fourth Gospel another episode is described in chapter 7. Here the author states that Jesus traveled in Galilee after his disputes with his relatives in Nazareth. He did not want to travel in Judea because "the Jews there were waiting to kill him" (Jn. 7:1). The feast of tabernacles was near "so Jesus' brothers said to him: 'Leave this place and go to Judea so that your disciples will see the works you are doing. No one hides what he is doing if he wants to be well known. Since you are doing these things, let the whole world know about you.'" It is clear that this passage was intended by the author to be read with heavy sarcasm. To make that crystal clear, John adds a parenthetical explanation. "For not even his brothers believed in him!" Jesus declined this challenge, saying that the time was not right for him. He suggested that they go up to the feast, but he would remain in Galilee. After his brothers went up without him, Jesus apparently changed his mind and also went up, but in secret until he began to teach publicly. It is a trip to Jerusalem about which the synoptic gospels seem to know nothing.

There is certainly nothing in these passages or anywhere else in the Gospels that would indicate any relationship of trust or support between Jesus and his family, especially between Jesus and his brothers. Even at the cross where the Fourth Gospel suggests that Jesus' mother stood at a distance watching, the evangelist has Jesus commend his mother to the care of the beloved disciple. Surely if a brother had been there, that would not have been necessary.

There is no hint in any Gospel narrative that during

the lifetime of Jesus any member of Jesus' family, including James, his brother, was ever close or understanding or sensitive to him. He, like the others, appeared questioning, perhaps embarrassed, scoffing, unimpressed, certainly unconverted.

I suspect that impressing your next oldest brother is among the more difficult tasks in life. We are deeply aware in our psychologically oriented world of sibling rivalry, though some knowledge of it has certainly existed since the time of the legendary Cain and Abel. The rivalry is most intense between the first two children in a family and especially if they are of the same sex. I have a younger brother whom I admire in his adulthood a great deal, but when we were children, the rivalry between us was real. In many ways he is lucky to be alive today. He bears the marks of "brotherly love," a scar on top of his head, a broken arm, a deviated septum, a broken nose. I suppose in many ways we still compete, though I find now that my intense pride in him outweighs every other emotion. He too is an Episcopal priest, and I can honestly say the best sermon I have ever heard in my life was delivered by him. Lest the reader think I escaped this juvenile warfare unscathed, let me say that I bear a few scars myself, including a broken arm; but my two-year advantage in age rendered him more often the victim.

A public career such as the one that marked the life of Jesus of Nazareth must have been very hard on his family. When people began to question the sanity of one member of the family, the public reputation of all members was suddenly at stake. To have the attitude of the next oldest brother in the family of Joseph and Mary be one of critical scoffing, cynical negativity would be the easiest thing in the world to understand.

To have that same brother become a disciple, to call Jesus Lord, and to assume a position of leadership in the Christian movement would be a radical departure indeed. It would represent an internal revolution of major proportions. It might even be called a miracle. But that is what happened after the Moment of Easter.

When Paul, writing to the Corinthians in A.D. 56, gives a list of the resurrection appearances, he states, "Then he appeared to James" (1 Cor. 15:7). The only James Paul ever referred to is James, the Lord's brother. This is a resurrection tradition that no Gospel correlates, but it is obvious that something happened to James, the Lord's brother, which called him first into discipleship and finally into the major responsibility of leadership of the Christian movement. Let me trace the biblical evidence that supports this.

In the Epistle to the Galatians, written in A.D. 49–50, Paul is involved in a polemic. The gospel he has been preaching has been compromised by the behavior of the Galatians. Paul reviews his call to apostleship, his days of persecution, his conversion, his trip to Arabia, and finally his trip to Jerusalem to get information from Peter with whom the account says he stayed for two weeks. Then he adds, "But I saw none of the other apostles except James, the Lord's brother" (Gal. 1:19). Apostle is the title applied by Paul to James, the Lord's brother. This is to say that James' apostleship was acknowledged in A.D. 49, while Paul was still defending his right to be called by that title.

In the same Epistle (Gal. 2:9) Paul goes on to say that James, Peter, and John seemed to be the leaders, "who were reputed to be pillars" in Jerusalem and that they recognized his special ministry. Note the order: James is listed first. Clearly, this is still James, the Lord's brother. In Galatians 2:12, James is again mentioned as the one who sent emissaries from Jerusalem to check on Peter's enjoying table fellowship with the Gentiles.

When we shift to the Lukan history in the book of Acts, we find these intriguing references. Luke describes the group of people gathered in Jerusalem following the Resurrection and Ascension as they waited for the coming of the promised Spirit. He includes in his list Mary, the mother of Jesus, and his brothers. Already, Luke asserts, the family of Jesus was at that early moment numbered with the disciples. Later in the book of Acts (Acts 15:1ff.), the first council of the churches was called to deal with the manner in which Gentiles were to be incorporated into the church. The final solution was worked out and offered by James, the Lord's brother (Acts 15:13). There is one other reference in Acts 21:18 where Paul once again went to Jerusalem to confer with James. Clearly, James was the leading figure and the leading power in the Jerusalem Christian community.

It is difficult to base any argument on the Epistle of James, for before doing that one must go to great length to establish the authorship and to date the work, which is outside the scope of this volume. It is interesting a note that John A. T. Robinson in his book *Dating the New Testament* suggests that it is a very early book, maybe the earliest in the New Testament, and from the pen of James the Just, the Lord's brother. This book, however, has not been positively received in New Testament circles. At the very least, we can say that this epistle purports to be true to the tradition of James. In any event this epistle does refer to Jesus the Christ as Lord, and the author James calls himself Jesus' servant. The Epistle of Jude purports to be written by Jude, the brother of James and another brother of Jesus. Whether these last two references can be substantiated or not, we can be certain of the fact that the brothers of Jesus were not impressed, were not followers of Jesus during his lifetime. They were scoffers, cynics, suspicious of Jesus' sanity.

But something happened. Paul says it happened at Easter, and James, the brother of the Lord, moved into discipleship and into leadership of the Christian Church. Look at James before Easter. Look at James after Easter. What caused a change that was this dramatic?

One final note: There is an apocryphal Gospel of James, some fragments of which have been preserved. In it the author attempts to place some content into the Pauline notation that the risen Christ appeared to James. It is interesting that this author says that when the resurrected Jesus appeared to James, he invited him into communion with him in these words: "Come, my brother, prepare a table, and I will break bread with you."

That is the witness of James, the brother of the Lord. It is a bit more speculative, but its weight must be added to the total testimony.

Chapter 8

A New Holy Day

I call an expert witness who will testify as to the power of the Jewish Sabbath.

One of the most important worship traditions of the Jewish people was the observance of the seventh day of the week as the Sabbath. This was more than just a custom by the time of the life of Jesus—it was part of the Jewish identity. Its power had a deep emotional hold upon the lives of the people. This power was primarily a result of the period of the Babylonian exile from 597 B.C. to 538 B.C.

The Sabbath day of rest seems to have had its most ancient origin as a monthly festival of the new moon. Much later, under the influence of the Sumerians who adopted a seven-day week, the Sabbath evolved into a one-day-each-week festival. It was, however, at this time not related to the creation story. That was to come much later.

In the Deuteronomic version of the Ten Commandments (Deut. 5) written perhaps centuries before but serving as a basis for King Josiah's Deuteronomic reformation in 621 B.C., the injunction to rest on the Sabbath day was related to a Hebrew passion against human or animal exploitation that appears to be a far earlier tradition than the creation story. Rest, according to Deuteronomy, was a right to be demanded, not a privilege to be extended. Do not forget, said the Deuteronomic writer, that you were slaves in Egypt subject to exploitation, so every seventh day every creature has the right to rest from labor. This, however, did not have the force of law, and the Sabbath observance had been generally abandoned until the period of the exile.

In 598 B.C. the little nation of Judah was attacked by the Babylonians under the command of King Nebuchadrezzar. The outnumbered Jewish army, following the historic pattern of defense in this area, had retreated into fortress Jerusalem where they held out for months until food and water gave out and they were forced to surrender. In keeping with Babylonian policy for dealing with conquered people, a massive population shift was ordered. Many of the able-bodied Jewish men, women, and children were sent on a long march into captivity in Babylon, and non-Jewish people were brought in to resettle the land. This policy seemed to the Babylonians to destroy future rebellion and to keep at a minimum nationalistic feelings against Babylon in the conquered provinces. When Assyria had employed this policy in 721 B.C. against the northern ten tribes of Israel, the result had been the loss of national identity, miscegenation, a gradual melding of Israel into the bloodstream of Middle Eastern peoples. The exiled tribes of the Northern Kingdom disappeared as a recognizable entity from the face of the earth and came to be known as the ten lost tribes of Israel.

This was well known to the Jewish leaders of the

New Holy Day

Southern Kingdom who were transported into the
Babylonian exile, among whom was the prophet–priest
Ezekiel. These leaders determined that for the sake of
the historic survival of their nation, they must maintain
the separateness and the identity of the Jewish people.
The chosen people must not vanish. No matter how
long it took, they must return to their holy land.
Hence, they set out deliberately to create a nationalistic
awareness that would survive separation from their
homeland for perhaps several generations.

Two symbols of their past they resurrected and rein-
stalled into the consciousness of their people as the
identifying signs of their Jewishness. Both symbols had
fallen into general disuse. They were the rite of circumcision and the Sabbath day observance. By these
two symbols they sought first to place the unmistakable
sign of Judaism on the body of every male Jew and
secondly they sought to segregate the whole people
from the society by making them look and act dif-
ferently on the seventh day of every week. They invested these two traditions with emotions, history, and
nationalistic fervor.

They rewrote or edited their scriptures to undergird
this new practice. The seven-day creation story of Gen-
esis 1:1–2:4 was edited into the existing traditions at
this time and placed at the opening of the written account of their sacred history. They edited such stories
as the manna in the wilderness narrative to allow for
the Sabbath to be observed properly (Ex. 16:29). On
the sixth day the children of Israel gathered twice the
daily supply of manna so they could refrain from gathering on the seventh day and thereby not violate the
prohibition against work. In every way possible the
Sabbath day observance was heightened by the exiled

people. It was part of the way the conquered nation resisted even in captivity their conqueror. It was a mark of both worship and patriotism—two powerful emotions. More and more precisely the meaning of this day was interpreted and the restrictions of this day defined.

When Judah did return many years later from the exile under the leadership of Zerubbabel, the nationalistic consciousness was even more enhanced. With the next century and a half Nehemiah, a Jewish Persian governor, and more especially, Ezra, a scribe, taught that the Babylonian exile had been God's punishment upon Israel for not keeping the law and the traditions rigidly enough. They sought to purge the nation of alien influences and weak-willed religious resolve. It was almost a nation reborn with only religious zealots for citizens. The sacredness of the Sabbath and the proper observance of the Sabbath were at the head of the list of how good Jews defined their Jewishness. A theocratic state was created in which the laws of the religious tradition became the laws of the state. The emotional appeal of the Sabbath was immense. It was like the American flag, motherhood, Sunday blue laws, and God all rolled into one.

The Jews spelled out quite explicitly the Sabbath day restrictions. Thirty-nine different kinds of work were specifically prohibited. You could not embalm the dead on the Sabbath. This prohibition is acted out in the resurrection narrative. The deaths of the victims of crucifixion were hastened by breaking the legs of the thieves and hurling the spear into Jesus' side. They were quickly removed from the cross and buried without the normal preparation of the bodies. The first moment in which they could embalm the body was dawn on the first day of the week, and for this purpose the women went to the tomb carrying the spices of embalmment.

One could not minister healing arts to a chronic disease or set a broken bone unless life itself was threatened. Jesus healed the man with the withered hand on the Sabbath and incurred the wrath of the religious establishment. A withered hand is a chronic situation. It would not have hurt anyone to wait until the first day of the week, his opponents argued. Criminals were not arrested on the Sabbath. That was unnecessary work. It was a day of relative sanctuary for outlaws. This also, I believe, becomes a factor in the resurrection narrative, making it unnecessary at least for all of the disciples to flee Jerusalem, for on the Sabbath they did not fear arrest.

You could not walk more than two thousand cubits, or three-fifths of a mile, without breaking the Sabbath. Two thousand cubits was the distance a priest had to walk in the temple to do his Sabbath duties. So that much walking became regarded as *a Sabbath day's journey* and was allowed. To go beyond that violated the Sabbath. The book of Acts (Acts 1:12) refers to the Mount of Olives as "a Sabbath day's journey" from Jerusalem. This also becomes a factor that may have impeded escape from Jerusalem for the disciples after the crucifixion and may support Luke and John's contention that suggested that at least some of the disciples remained in Jerusalem until the first day of the week after the crucifixion.

The observance of this day was rigidly codified, and these rules were written into civil law as well as religious observance. The Sabbath was a deeply emotional, religious, national, patriotic mark of Jewish identity. It had an enormous hold upon the people. It was among the most sacred and the best observed of the traditions of Judaism. No one who knows anything about tradition, religious custom, the resistance to change of emotionally held, pious practices can overestimate the power of the Sabbath. When anything or anyone arises to minimize or to challenge the power of that tradition, the response will be less than rational.

We joke about this constantly. There is always the story of the lady who said, "If the King James Bible was good enough for Jesus, it is good enough for me." Every major church that attempts to change its liturgy confronts an angry, emotional response from many devout worshipers. I remember well a lady with dyed red hair who was the self-appointed guardian of traditional liturgical practices in a small eastern North Carolina town where I spent eight very special years. She monitored everything I did and never hesitated to tell me what I did wrong. I turned on the lights my first Maundy Thursday night, not knowing that this parish always celebrated Maundy Thursday in the dark. By my first Easter I had accumulated about twenty black marks in her book, and when it rained on Easter and prevented us from having our traditional sunrise service in the churchyard, she exploded. Confronting me in the cloister, she exclaimed, "It never rained on Easter until you became our rector!"

People are emotional, irrational, and deeply committed to the worship traditions of their lives. One of the holiest and most emotional religious traditions of the Jews was the proper observance of the Sabbath day. It was deep-seated, touching all of the nerve ends of their lives. All of the disciples and all of the women who followed the disciple band were Jews deeply related to this worship pattern and tradition.

Yet something happened in the lives of these people, something profound, life-changing, and emotional. This something is identified by Paul and all the Gospel writers with the first day of the week. This identification gave birth to a new holy day for worship. Christian Sunday and Jewish Sabbath were not the same. Christian Sunday was *not* the Christian version of the Sabbath, at least not when the tradition of the first day of the week was born. They have different meanings, different origins, different characters. The perhaps inevitable blending of the two days in history has diminished our awareness of just how powerful and how strikingly new the choice by the Christians of the first day of the week as their holy day really was.

The first day of the week was the day of the Resurrection, the day God acted. The Sabbath was the seventh day of the week, the day God rested. Christians observed the first day of the week by festivity and celebration. The phrase *a celebration of the Holy Communion* was derived from the basic character of this day. On the other hand, the Jewish Sabbath was observed with solemnity and by refraining from labor. So deeply have the two days been blended that many people grow up feeling that Sunday carries with it a prohibition against working. But in fact there is not one verse of holy writ that suggests that one should not work on Sunday. The confusion of the Jewish Sabbath with the Christian Sunday was a much later development and is still used today in an attempt to keep community blue laws operative. Sunday blue laws may be pointed toward a noble goal, but using an inappropriate biblical text to support them is hardly a noble tactic. Sunday was different from the Sabbath. It was special, dramatic, a *new* holy day, a new worship tradition.[6]

All of the Gospels and Paul locate the first experience of Easter on the third day or the first day of the week. By A.D. 56, according to Paul's letter to the Corinthians (1 Cor. 16:2), Sunday, the first day of the week, was established and kept as "the Lord's Day." In Acts 20:7 Luke records the fact that the members of the Christian community were in the custom and habit of assembling on the first day of the week for the uniquely Christian worship act of breaking bread together. The Fourth Gospel indicates that the disciples' first experience of Easter took place on the first day of the week following the crucifixion. This was the occasion, we are told, when Thomas was not present. No further experiences of the Easter Moment occurred, says the Fourth Gospel, until "after eight days," or according to the way the Jews counted time, this would mean the first day of the second week. John appears to be asserting that what happened on the first day of the first week was so exciting, so powerful, so life-changing that the first day of every week was changed into a day on which the Moment of Easter was reenacted. By the time of the book of Revelation (Rev. 1:10), *the Lord's Day* is a clear synonym for Sunday. In the apocryphal Epistle of Barnabas, the author asserts, "From the earliest times Christians kept the first day of the week as the day upon which Jesus rose from the dead."

There is little doubt that a new holy day was created from the Easter Moment, a day that rivaled and in time replaced the most sacred worship tradition of the Jews. That is an event of momentous power. What does it take to create a new holy day? What does it take for people raised in the Sabbath day tradition of the Jews to move away ever so slightly from the observance of that day? What does it take first to admit the Christian Sunday alongside the Jewish Sabbath and then to watch it replace the Sabbath in their emotions?

Let us not forget the Jewishness of the first disciples and of Paul, the former pupil of Gamaliel. The energy it takes to develop a new holy day, a new worship tradition, is enormous. Where did that energy come from? Here is an effect that can be measured, an historic phenomenon that can be studied. It exists in history and time, but it points to an originating moment that may have been beyond time or history. Feel its power. Listen to its witness. Weigh its evidence.

The witness steps down.

Chapter 9

The Oneness of God Expands

I call a member of the Jewish priestly class to the witness stand. My purpose will be to examine the power of the central theological claim of the Jews that God is One, Holy, Other.

At the heart and center of the faith of Israel is the Shema. "Hear, O Israel, the Lord your God is one Lord." It is followed by the injunction that you shall have no other gods before him. The oneness of God did not develop instantaneously, and it was not always the same high and lofty concept even for the Jews; but it was distinctly a Jewish contribution to the developing theological thought of the world. The God of Israel was first and foremost a God who acted in history. Israel was born as a result of the deliverance from Egypt. That birth was established at Sinai. That deliverance could not be understood apart from the Jews' sense of Yahweh who took up their cause against their enemies. This God elected Israel. This God endowed a slave people with the special status of the chosen people. He covenanted with them at Sinai, revealed his will to them in the Torah, and called them to respond.

A God of history differs dramatically from a God of nature. The God of history has no abode on a mountain or in the sky. He cannot be identified with the sun or the moon. He cannot be imaged in things made with hands. No idol could capture his essence for the mind of Israel; hence idols were forbidden. His holy name could not even be spoken by his own people, for to the Jewish people to call the name of God was to have some semblance of control over God. God was mystery, power, unpredictability for the Jew; therefore, his name could not even be uttered by the worshiper. "Your ways are not my ways, says the Lord" (Is. 55:8). God was one. God was holy. God was other. He could be met, engaged, wrestled with, followed, but he could never be captured, tamed, domesticated, or controlled.

The one natural symbol used for God was the wind—Ruach—the Spirit of God which was without beginning or end. One could see the effects of God as one could see the effects of the wind; but God, like the wind, was invisible, uncontrollable, not to be discerned by the finite minds of men or women. God could only be pointed to, and where he had been could be seen, never where he was going.

God knew no national boundaries for the Jews. He was universal, and as this insight grew, the national gods of Israel's neighbors were seen as idols. The Jews struggled with this, falling away from time to time, so different was this idea from the prevailing thought forms of their day, but finally in Judaism this concept persisted. At least one psalmist (Psalm 137), when he was carried away from the sacred soil of Judah into

Babylonian captivity, wondered how he could "sing the Lord's song in a strange land," but the exiled people learned that they could. Indeed, in the writings of the unknown prophet of the exile we call Second Isaiah (Is. 40–55), the universal oneness of Yahweh reaches what is for me the highest and the holiest point in the Old Testament.

The Jewish passion against idolatry shaped and formed the national personality of the Jewish people. The Holy God Yahweh demanded worship and justice. Ethical monotheism became the theological word for describing Judaism. It fueled the ministry of the prophets. Idolatry was the worship of a god who had eyes but who could not see, ears but who could not hear. That is, the god who was an idol could not demand that one's worship and one's behavior had to be in harmony. For Israel, worship was human justice being offered to God. Justice was divine worship being acted out. Idolatry was the separation of the one from the other. When this was expressed liturgically, it meant that God was not limited to time or space, or to a shrine or a temple. No place was apart from God's all-seeing eye, so no image of God could be erected anywhere. God could not be bound to images made with hands.

In the national character of Israel, this idea was their cross and their crown. Frequently, it was read by the other nations as a kind of religious arrogance. Other peoples felt the Jews to be denigrating, even spitting on their gods, and they reacted in expected ways. But at the same time the oneness, holiness, and otherness of God for the Jewish people was woven deep into their psyches and became a mark of their Jewishness. This was heightened in the period of the exile when a deliberate effort was made by this conquered folk to identify and to celebrate the differences that set Jews apart from all others. Circumcision was revived. A rigid Sabbath day observance was enforced. Finally, it became a mark of Judaism that they would never bow their heads to anything or anyone, save God alone. When the Jews returned from exile under Nehemiah and Ezra, these three factors achieved the level of national consciousness.

Attacking armies found the Jews easy to conquer but hard to subdue. They were a weak and pitiful military force but a stiff-necked defeated people to administer. The accolade *stiff-necked* referred very specifically to their unwillingness to bow their heads before any power, temporal or spiritual, save Yahweh alone. This became a particular problem when the Roman armies swept over the empire and replaced the Macedonians. An important part of the Roman practice to build cohesiveness in the empire was accomplished by requiring a religious unity that was centered in the worship, or at the very least, in the reverence of the Caesar. To most conquered peoples this was a fairly simple, generally inoffensive symbol of their status and afforded no real problem. However, this decree struck at the very heart of the Jewishness of the Jew. "Bow our heads to Caesar? Never!" This was their clear response.

At first Rome was perplexed. This tiny province, which had so little to commend itself, certainly had no power to back up this seditious behavior. A small show of force is all it would take, the leaders thought. So the orders came down. "Bow your head to Caesar or face execution for treason." The Jews met this by preparing to be executed. Some were, and the Jews still did not relent. Finally, it began to dawn on the Roman authorities that these peculiar people because of some religious scruples would all die before acquiescing in the Roman practice requiring subject people to bow their heads to Caesar. So this tiny, militarily impotent nation won a concession from mighty Rome. Alone of all conquered peoples Judah was exempt from the requirement of bowing to Caesar. It was a small victory, but it revealed very deeply the religious fervor and the power by which the concept of the oneness, the holiness, the otherness of God had captured the Jewish people.

In A.D. 26 a new young Roman procurator named Pontius Pilate was appointed ruler of the conquered province of Judah. Not yet experienced in dealing with the religious sensitivities of his Jewish subjects, Pilate in a show of force had his Roman soldiers parade through the streets of Jerusalem wearing medallions bearing the sacred image of the Divine Caesar. Instead of intimidating the Jewish people into acquiescence and reverence before the imperial power of Rome, this action created a religious riot which Pilate had to put down with force. Pilate was reprimanded by Rome but not removed. But some four years later, this episode helps to explain some of the behavior attributed to Pilate during Holy Week. Indeed, his very presence in Jerusalem at the time of the Passover was a precautionary move to guarantee no more blemishes on his record. His normal place of residence was Caesarea, named, of course, for his chief of state.

As the Gospel narratives reveal, this Jewish attitude toward God permeated and governed the relationship the disciples had with Jesus before the Easter Moment. Jesus was the master, the teacher, the leader, but there is no instance that would indicate that Jesus had become the object of veneration, or adoration, or worship. He rebuked the disciples, and the disciples rebuked Jesus. They took their arguments to him. They loved him, admired him, got exasperated with him, misunderstood him, tried to force his hand, begged him to explain his parables, reveled in their status as his followers—but they never seem to have considered worshiping him.

Even at Caesarea Philippi when Peter made the startling confession, "You are the Christ, the Son of the Living God," he was really saying, "You are the Messiah" (*Mashiah* in Hebrew)—a title that did not carry with it divine connotations. You are the expected deliverer of Israel, the promised one. On the lips of Peter, "Son of the Living God" was not a description of divinity or of God's paternity. All faithful Jews were called *sons of the Living God*.[7] This became perfectly obvious when Jesus commended Peter for his answer and began to inform Peter and the others about what it meant to be the Christ. Peter's response was to correct and argue with Jesus. That is hardly an appropriate reply if he had just acknowledged Jesus' divine origins. Clearly, Peter had not done that. In this period of time the primary connotation of *son* was not paternity as we seem to think, but obedience. A true son was one obedient to the will of the father regardless of his paternity. Words we think are self-evident are frequently not self-evident at all, even so simple a word as son.

Had there been any concept among the disciples that Jesus was *the Son of God* in the sense that this phrase came to be understood in the Hellenistic world or as we use those words theologically today, then the behavior of the disciples was nonsensical. What we call the divinity of Christ simply did not exist in the minds of the disciples before the Easter Moment. By his disciples he was betrayed, denied, forsaken. When it came down to saving Jesus or themselves, they voted unanimously for themselves. There is nothing in the pre-Easter account of the behavior of those associated with Jesus that would indicate in any way that they regarded him as divine or as the object of worship—nothing!

Then something happened. The Easter Moment dawned. And in that Moment the concept of God, the deep belief locked in the very fibre of every Jew and for which they were always willing to die if need be, expanded dramatically—virtually exploded, erupted like a great volcano. Something happened to these Jews who had known Jesus that forced them to change and to change radically. Throwing over everything they had known and been before, discarding their ancient heritage, abandoning what had seemed to be sanity and common sense, they *saw,* they *knew* Jesus in terms of God and God in terms of Jesus. Jesus was not merely venerated, or studied, or respected and followed as the founder and chief teacher of a new religion. He was proclaimed as *alive;* he was worshiped as the very essence of God; he was in a wondrous new way a living presence at work among those who had known him. An extraordinary and revolutionary idea was born. Christians came to realize that Jesus himself led his followers and the whole Christian community—miraculously and truly—through his Spirit.

From the Moment of Easter Jesus was included in the worship of God. They began to address their prayers to Jesus. It was an incredible, instantaneous theological revolution. The followers of Jesus began to say the most astonishing things about him—and the things they said were made all the more astonishing by the fact that they were Jews. Our minds are dulled to the ecstatic quality of the revolution the New Testament contains because we have for so long been accustomed to these theological words attributing divinity to Jesus, but they were radical revolutionary words when they were first uttered. Remember that Paul was brought up in the strict pharisaic tradition of Judaism, and yet Paul could call Jesus "Lord of both the dead and the living" (Rom. 14:9). "He was of the very nature of God" (Phil. 2:6), so that "at the name of Jesus every knee should bow, in heaven and on earth and under the earth, and every tongue confess that Jesus Christ is Lord, to the glory of God the Father" (Phil. 2:10–11). These are astonishing words to flow from the lips of a Jew. They are words that require a revolution in thought, and that revolution demands an explanation—an explanation that clearly must focus on the Moment of Easter, for that is when the revolution occurred.

There are numerous other battle cries of the revolution. The book of Acts tells us that Saul of Tarsus was commissioned to bring back from Damascus all who "call upon this Name" (Acts 9:14). If Acts is accurate at this point and if Paul's conversion can be dated as Adolf von Harnack does within one year of the events of Holy Week, then clearly prayers addressed to Jesus were a very early Christian phenomenon. The story of Stephen's martyrdom also includes such a prayer. The ecstatic cry of Thomas in the Fourth Gospel places the revolution of the Jewish understanding of God in its most blatant form. Thomas says to Jesus, "My Lord and my God," unbelievable words to escape the lips of a Jew.[8]

Something happened to the consciousness of Jewish

people in the Moment of Easter that was so real, so dramatic, so powerful, so life-changing, so mind-altering that they had to struggle to find the words that could express their experience. They knew that the deepest worship tradition of Israel had been expanded. They knew that somehow the oneness, the holiness, the otherness of God had from that moment on to include Jesus of Nazareth. They knew that never again could they envision God without Jesus, never again could they see Jesus without seeing God. This revolution took place in Judaism where every bit of their history and every shred of their tradition would be against it.

We can measure the effects of this revolution. They demand an exploration into the cause. Revolutions do not occur just because someone thinks they would be a good idea. Revolutions erupt with enormous power. This is as true of revolutions in theology as it is of political revolutions. To worship Jesus as Lord, to see Jesus as of the essence of God, to direct prayers to Jesus is a revolution. For all this to occur before Christianity moves out of the womb of Judaism is astonishing. The power of the Easter Moment is staggering. It demands exploration.

The witness steps down. We are left to weigh the power of his testimony.

Chapter 10

Judea, Scripture, and Paul

The trial is over. The major testimony has been presented. The impact of Easter has been measured, experienced, looked at, weighed. There are other things that could be presented. They are not different, perhaps they are not capable of being isolated from the main thrust of our witnesses, but they do add another angle of vision, an additional shaft of light. Because of this they may help to expand the witness, fill in a gap here and there, and strengthen the sense that Easter was a mighty moment affecting history so dramatically that some explanation is required.

When we try to embrace the fact that all of Christian history—its moments of glory and its times of depravity, its art, its music, its architecture, its religious certainty that gave rise to inquisitions and anti-Semitism, its institutions, its political power—can be traced back to a single moment we call Easter, then the enormity of that Moment can be properly appreciated. Take Easter away, and history is robbed of more than any one of us can imagine, whether we be Christian or not. So we try to organize and place in rational form some of the immediate effects that flowed from that moment and created the movement that shaped our world. To that primary evidence presented in this section, I now add a few secondary notes to round out the picture.

First, to the best of my knowledge, it is not questioned that Christianity broke out in human history in Jerusalem rather then in some remote region of Galilee. No matter where scholars finally conclude the Easter Moment was first experienced, there is no doubt that Jerusalem is the city in which Christianity was born. This meant that from the very beginning Christianity had to contend with those whose vested interests were not well served by this movement. If Christianity had been a tender plant liable to destruction, the power arrayed against it in Jerusalem alone might well have destroyed it. If there was any way this new faith could have been discredited, the religious hierarchy had ample reason and opportunity to want to do so. If the Easter Moment was a hoax, if some alternative explanation could have been found for what the disciples were claiming was the Resurrection of their Lord, Jerusalem would have offered the best opportunity. Yet none of these things happened. Instead, the religious hierarchy responded with telling persecution. No one ever persecutes what can be discredited. You only persecute that which threatens you. Jerusalem as the locale for the dawn of the Christian movement gives it a bit more authenticity, for Jerusalem was the locale of the most intense opposition.

Second, it must be noted that very quickly the words, the teachings, and the parables of Jesus were seen in a new light. Healing stories, nature miracle stories, and stories about Jesus began to be gathered. Before the end of that decade the passion narratives that carry Jesus' story from Palm Sunday to Easter began to achieve a written unity. But the passion story makes no sense without Easter. Take Easter away, and it portrays a disaster. Never would this story have entered the memory of humanity. Without Easter, it is the story of complete failure and shameful death.

Yet in the power of the Moment of Easter, the followers of Jesus gathered it, preserved it, revered it, and clung to each spectacular detail of the narrative, for Easter turned that story of defeat into a prelude to a new vision, a new reality. It ceased to be a tragedy. In time, the passion story became the center of even larger gospels. But it is important to note that the disciples began not only to proclaim the gospel of Jesus, but they also proclaimed Jesus as the gospel. The proclaimer was made the content of the proclamation. Without this, Matthew, Mark, Luke, and John would not have been written.

Nothing about the teaching of Jesus inspired a written account during his earthly existence. His teaching is even now not judged as particularly original in content. Joachim Jeremias, a noted Bible scholar, suggests that the unique thing about the teaching of Jesus is his application of the intimate familial Aramaic word *Abba* to God. Almost everything else about his teaching, Jeremias declares, can be found in the Old Testament or the Talmud or the Midrash. But Easter revealed a reality about Jesus that infused the words and events of his life with enormous power. Beyond the fact of his death had come a Moment that caused the stories to be gathered and later to be published, for this life was its own gospel. Easter was the moment when the power that reinterpreted the life of this Jesus was to be met and engaged. The biblical witness is clear.

Finally, the conversion of Saul of Tarsus to be Paul the missionary apostle was a moment of some substance for the Christian Church. There is no question that Saul was a learned Jew, well connected and trusted by the Jewish authorities. Yet his conversion was total, dramatic, and complete. Surely the critics of the Christian movement must have wondered how that movement could capture a man of Paul's credentials and capabilities.

This entire section has been designed not to prove resurrection. That is beyond the scope of this reasoning process. It is only to identify historic, measurable effects that can be observed and that apparently flow from the Moment we call Easter. Lives were changed dramatically. A dispirited, scattered, cowardly band of men was reconstituted, galvanized, energized into a powerful missionary force. A family moved from scoffing criticism into the very leadership of the movement. A new holy day was born. The historic theological understanding of God that had marked the national character of the Jewish people was radically redefined. Stories and accounts of this Jesus were understood in new ways and began to be collected. Jesus himself was seen as the content of the gospel that they proclaimed. Jerusalem was the locale where this movement erupted, and a leading member of the anti-Christian religious establishment joined the Christian movement, enabling it to leap even the boundaries of Judaism and to emerge onto the stage of the world.

All of this is historic data that begs for an adequate definition and points us dramatically to the Easter Moment. We now turn to that Moment and with all the tools of biblical scholarship and contemporary understanding available to us will try to penetrate its meaning and experience its power.

Part III

Exploring the Easter Moment

Chapter II

Introduction

Something happened! Easter was the name by which that something came to be known. It was determinative in the birth of the Christian movement and therefore crucial for all of Western civilization. No moment of world history carries with it such power, such a measure of our destiny, such yearning. The Moment of Easter is the watershed for Christians. The whole structure of the church, its faith, and its belief hangs here. If there is no eternal, unshakable, life-giving truth behind the words that purport to describe that Moment of Easter, then Christianity collapses into a pious hope, a false dream, and even a cruel delusion.

So much rides on Easter. The hopes of countless generations are attached to this Moment. The courage that ennobled lives and that banished the fear of death is attached to the resurrection faith. So not surprisingly when one probes Easter with honesty and with the best scholarship available to us, he or she ploughs a field of intense threat, tension, and anxiety. The insecure of faith will scream that such a study undermines belief, raises doubts. But an insecure faith is no faith at all. When one's belief has to be protected from honest inquiry, it is clear that one's faith has already died. There is a vast difference between believing in God and believing *in believing* in God. The threat, the fear, the defensiveness always arises out of the latter.

In this section I invite my readers to explore this revelatory Easter Moment. I invite you to dare to ask all of the probing, bold, and frightening questions that you can imagine. If the truth behind the Easter Moment collapses, none of us will be the worse for it unless we consider it good to live by delusion. But if we discover a reality that cannot be shaken, a truth that invites us to live on new levels, then we can confront our skeptical world as honest believers with an integrity that obviously has power. That integrity marked previous generations of Christians, but theirs was not a nonbelieving age like ours. The reward of honesty, integrity, and commitment that lies at the end of such a journey is worth the risk involved. Indeed, our age requires it.

The probe of Easter must come from within the community of faith. We are the ones who must raise the difficult questions. Is resurrection true? Can it be true? Does Easter represent that which is real, or was it created because we human beings desperately needed it to be real? Is there a certainty on which our deepest hopes are fastened, or are we who say we believe just pretending because we cannot face life without an Easter in it?

Our method in this section will be to explore every shred of evidence we can find, to peel back the layers of the record until we have come as close to the Easter Moment itself as possible. When that destination has been reached, then the test will be whether or not we can enter that Moment, share in it, make it a part of our lives. For if Easter is real, it is also timeless and eternal and available to us as fully as it was available to the disciples.

The layers before us are obvious. Something happened. Someone experienced it. Someone tried to put what was experienced into words, both oral and written. Then the words themselves took on a life of their own. They were told and retold, added to and subtracted from, translated and retranslated, collated and systematized, preached on, expounded, clarified. Like all words, the words about Easter did not capture or exhaust the meaning of the event they purported to describe. Words are symbols. They point to truth. They do not capture truth. We have to use words; we have nothing else to use. But when words are employed, distortion is inevitable. We must see these limitations before we can begin to probe beyond the limitations. Words are windows through which we look to explore the ultimate truth of life.

I come out of that school of theology that believes theological certainty is a vice, not a virtue. Theology can never be ultimate. It is a human attempt to give rational form to that which is ultimate. Those who pretend to possess certainty, or unchanging truth, or *the faith once delivered to the saints* seem to me to be playing a game called *Let's Pretend*.

"Let's pretend that our small human minds can embrace the ultimate mystery of God."

"Let's pretend that our finite words can capture the infinite truth of God."

"Let's pretend that God is so small or so manageable that He (a strangely symbolic human and distorting pronoun to use for God) will fit into that system of thought that I erect for God, a system of thought that affirms me and thus enables me to rest secure in my religious status and allows me to feel justified in my critical judgments of those who do not hold 'The Faith' in so pure a form as I." As a matter of fact, the use of the term *The Faith* implies that Christianity can be reduced to a set of agreed-on rational propositions that were dropped from heaven fully developed and complete with footnotes by C. B. Moss.[9] Anyone who knows even the slightest bit of the history of the development of Christian thought and doctrine knows how questionable such images are.

The theological fact that is clearest to me is that no human form can ever do more than point to the essence of God. The Bible, the creeds, doctrine, ecumenical councils, the papacy, every articulation of the Christian gospel is finally but a human form, a pointer, a symbol. When we elevate our forms into ultimacy and claim for them infallibility, we become idolatrous. In religious history this idolatry lies behind the bloodiest moments of our human story; for when any group of persons becomes convinced that they possess the ultimate truth, the imposition of that truth or the persecution of those who do not possess that truth becomes ever so justified.

Look at the history of the Christian Movement. It is not very noble. Inquisitions, heresy hunts, witch trials, violent anti-Semitism are but a few of the ugly scars that are always visible in that history, and demonically enough, these horrors are always administered in the name of the God of Love. It is no wonder that many people look at the dichotomy between what we Christians say and how we Christians have acted; and blinded by our forms, they never see our God.

Yet at the same time I am aware that for us human beings it is anxiety-producing to live without certainty, particularly in the area of religious belief. There is a constant temptation to which religious people regularly succumb, pretending that our human forms or formulations are ultimate. This temptation arises out of an insatiable human need for security. When one's security cannot be vested in that which is ultimate (God), it will be vested in that which is not ultimate (forms that attempt to capture or define God). There will always be those who are unable to live on the theological edge of uncertainty or unable to live on the inescapable human levels of insecurity. They will cling to their literal creeds or literal Bibles or ancient and unchanging traditions with a defensive intensity. Inevitably these people seem to believe that humility in those who face the ultimate mystery of God is symptomatic of not believing at all. They will misunderstand the absence of the arrogance of certainty, believing it to be the presence of a relativity that denies the ultimate. They will be threatened, and they will attack the searching, probing, theologically uncertain Christian in the name of their idolatrous theological security systems. Such attacks should be expected, welcomed, endured, and finally ignored.

I mention these things because I want us in this section to sink ourselves as deeply as we can into the forms in which our Lord's Resurrection was and is traditionally communicated. I hope this can be done without fear, defensiveness, or scaring the religiously insecure. I am convinced that the authoritarian stand of church bodies and church leaders has the primary result of closing the doors on serious religious searching for the masses of people in our generation. If our clergy and our churches would dare to lead the laity in a deep and honest search for the truth that is in Jesus, our Christ (a search that would lead us beyond every literalized symbol, every literal word), if the questions, the doubts, the fears of lay people could find expression inside the community of faith without judgment or criticism or condemnation, then I am convinced there would be a burst of life and energy in the church that would startle us. For anyone who lives fully in the twentieth century cannot be a man or woman of theological certainty, so vast is our world, our knowledge, our experience. One of the deepest needs that I find in human life today is the need to locate a community where life's ultimate questions may be asked and where honest answers may be probed using the full and valued resources of the church's long and significant heritage. Such a place would not employ the authoritarian clichés—*the Bible says* or *the church teaches*—to stifle the search for truth.

The best way I know to focus clearly on this truth is to recognize that if our Lord Jesus Christ had been incarnate in our day instead of at the dawn of the Christian era, we would have used vastly different words and concepts to speak about his truth. I presume that since truth is eternal, the incarnate Lord of the twentieth century would not have been different in essence from the incarnate Lord of the first century. But the twentieth century has a vastly different view of reality from that of the first century. Our world is not flat. We cannot talk glibly of up and down as those words relate to space. We do not accept a view of genetics that underlies the birth narratives of the New Testament. We do not ascribe epilepsy, deaf muteness, and schizo-phrenia to demon possession. These were common as-sumptions that first-century folk did not question, and, consequently, any great and mighty wonder that they experienced had to be understood in terms of their as-sumptions, their world view. To expect anything else is to be naïve. To literalize their world view as it comes to us in their attempt to explain how God was in this Christ is to be foolish.

There is a truth beyond the forms in which that truth is described and communicated. To point to that transcendent truth is our goal. To literalize the forms in which ultimate truth is described is to miss forever the opportunity for interaction with the truth. To iden-tify truth with the forms that communicate it is to fall prey to the distorting sin of literalization. To literalize words is to fail to see where they point.

In a way this is elementary, yet in the realm of re-ligion, this elementary insight is violated time after time in the religious assumptions of people whose com-mitments are genuinely deep, intensely personal, and profoundly emotional.

I would like to articulate in as definitive a way as possible my personal credo, my understanding of the Christian Gospel by which I seek to live. I want my readers to know the faith context out of which I am writing. Only then would I want to narrow our focus to examining the truth of Easter that lies behind the forms of the Easter narratives.

I believe that God is real and ultimate.

I believe that God shares in the qualities that lie be-hind the human word *personal*.

I believe that God is the source of life, the source of love, the infinite and inexhaustible ground of all being.

I believe that this ultimate and real God reveals himself in human history in ways that are both profound and mundane, but they always relate to what it means to be a person.

I believe that we, his creatures made in his image, are called to live in this world open to its infinite potential for life, love, and being.

I believe that in the historic life of Jesus of Nazareth, God was and is uniquely, dramatically, and decisively present in human history. In Jesus, God is met, engaged, revealed, worshiped.

I believe in the words of John A. T. Robinson that Jesus was the human face of God, living so deeply as to reveal the source of life, loving so completely as to reveal the source of love, being all that he was created to be so fully as to reveal the ground of all being. To say this as the Hebrews might have, using their verb theology rather than the ontological concepts of Greek philosophy, I believe that Jesus was and is God loving, God caring, God calling, God forgiving. Jesus is God revealing the infinite possibilities for human life beyond the barriers of our humanity that we erect to minister to our sense of alienation and insecurity.

I believe that Jesus is God breaking the ultimate barrier of time, space, finitude, and death—and inviting us to share in the wonder of an expanded transcendence even as we are caught up in the power of the life-giving Spirit we call holy. And yet that presence of God was lived out in that historic and fully human life we call Jesus.

When I read the New Testament and view in the Gospels and Epistles their attempt to reconstruct and to interpret that life, it is clear to me that the Easter Moment is the crucial, interpretive Moment of the entire drama. Whatever else Easter was, it was the Moment when human eyes were opened to see the full meaning of this Christ, to experience him, and to meet God in him in a way God had never been met before. So this is the Moment we need to examine beyond all other moments.

Chapter 12

Probing the Bible's Literal Level

Most people have no idea how to read the Bible. This is basically due to conscious and unconscious ideas and attitudes they hold toward the Bible. It is a caricature to say that many assume the Bible dropped from heaven fully written and usually in the King James Version; but more than one might want to suspect, such a view is not so far from the truth. For so many years the Bible was set apart from the common affairs of life that it developed its own mythologies. The tissue-thin, gold-edged pages, the print style of two columns on each page, the beautiful but archaic Elizabethan English, and the floppy leather cover all added to its mystique. I can remember as a child being reprimanded by my mother for placing something on top of the Bible. The Bible was always prominently displayed in our home, but I have no memory whatever of seeing or hearing it read. Important events like births and deaths were entered in it, but that seemed to be its only purpose so far as I was concerned.

In the average congregation of regular churchgoers, even the distinctions between the Gospels are far too subtle for most lay people to grasp. That is particularly obvious on the picture side of Christmas cards or in lawn crèche scenes when the shepherds and wise men are depicted together at the manger, a circumstance that no biblical data would support except by a blending process that the texts themselves would never support. Matthew, for example, who alone tells the wise men story, never knew the tradition of the manger or the story of no room for Mary and Joseph in the inn or the special census that compelled the holy family to go to Bethlehem. Matthew's sources assume, and his text accept the assumption that Mary and Joseph lived permanently in Bethlehem in a house, not a stable, and he further suggests that the magi might have arrived as much as two years after Jesus was born.

The most familiar folk knowledge about the Bible assumes a certain biographical order that begins with the birth of Jesus and progresses in an orderly narrative to his death and resurrection. The facts are that birth stories are given us only in Matthew and Luke, and their details are irreconcilable. Mark begins with Jesus' baptism; John begins with a theological, interpretive prologue and then moves to the adult life of Jesus. The only skeletal outline that can be discerned in Matthew, Mark, and Luke is that Jesus' public ministry began in Galilee and his crucifixion was in Jerusalem, and obviously it took a journey to get from one to the other. So basically these synoptic gospels have a Galilean phase, a journey phase, and a Jerusalem phase in their story of Jesus. Even this threadbare narrative outline is contradicted by the Fourth Gospel. The synoptics suggest a one-year public ministry, and the Fourth Gospel a three-year public ministry.

What the average lay person does not realize is that most of the material that is included in the Gospels existed in isolated vignettes without any time or space references in the oral period between the life and death of Jesus and the beginning of the era of written material. This oral tradition was kept alive by word-of-mouth transmission, and indeed the only part of the Jesus story that has an early narrative tradition is the passion account from Palm Sunday to Easter. The separate stories (pericope) were of several types: sayings of Jesus (sometimes with no context at all, sometimes with the briefest of contexts), miracle stories, stories about Jesus, and parables. These treasured accounts were like Christmas tree ornaments. Each was beautiful in and of itself, and each would fit onto the Christmas tree and add lustre to the whole no matter where it was placed. If Mark had written a year later and had arranged his separate vignettes in a different order, the story would not have been dramatically different.

This indeed happens among the separate Gospel authors. The miraculous catch of fish is told by Luke as an event in the early Galilean phase of Jesus' ministry, but in the Fourth Gospel it appears as a post-Resurrection narrative. Matthew, Mark, and Luke place the cleansing of the temple as an event of the last week of Jesus' life, part of the very climax itself, while the Fourth Gospel makes it an early event in the life of Jesus.

The most important fact to embrace about the Bible, however, is its historic context. Not one line, not a single verse of the New Testament is written except as a product of a community who lived in the power of Easter. Nothing was written during Jesus' life. No biographical detail is recorded except insofar as the post-Resurrection community demanded to know about the life and the teachings of the Risen One.

The stories of the Gospels are not biographies; they are proclamations about the Risen Christ. No Gospel writer tells infancy stories or childhood stories or ministry stories or records Jesus' words apart from an assumption of the events of Holy Week and Easter. The best and most overt symbol of this is that one-third of Mark and Matthew and forty percent of the Fourth Gospel are devoted to the events of the last one week in the life of Jesus. Only twenty-nine percent of Luke is devoted to the last one week, but that is probably accounted for by the later addition of Luke 1 and 2 to the corpus of this work. Chapter 3 of Luke with its elaborate dating system appears to be the original beginning of this work. The birth narratives are filled with words, phrases, and Hebraisms that appear nowhere else in Luke's writing and add weight to the suggestion that Luke took over a Palestinian Christmas pageant complete with metered hymns (Magnificat, Benedictus, Gloria in Excelsis, and Nunc Dimittis) and attached this profound and beautiful narrative to his Gospel account. Without the birth narratives Luke is in line with the other Gospels with thirty-five percent of his corpus being devoted to the last one week of Jesus' life.

The second obvious but not generally recognized fact is that no New Testament author assumed he was writing a piece of a larger volume to be called the New Testament. The unity the New Testament has is an imposed unity, imposed by the church as Christians grappled with the challenge that stemmed from a man named Marcion (A.D. 100–160) who had wanted to separate Christianity forever from its Hebrew and Old Testament roots. Marcion had drawn up a list of books and parts of books that he regarded as canonical. This forced church leaders to counter his influence by creating in effect a canon of Holy Scripture. There were many more Gospels than Matthew, Mark, Luke, and John, many more Epistles, more Acts-type books, and Revelation-type books than the twenty-seven finally recognized by the church as authoritative holy scripture.

The books chosen were not written at the same time or under the same circumstances. Perhaps a period as long as 100 years separated the first book of the New Testament to be written (either 1 Thessalonians or Galatians) from the last (2 Peter). The Gospels appear in our Bible first, but the fact remains that every epistle of Paul was written and Paul himself was dead before the first Gospel was written. It should also be noted that between the first Gospel (Mark) and the last Gospel (John), a period of perhaps 35 years elapsed.

When the books of the Bible are arranged chronologically, one can discern an historic progression and the growing apologetic needs of the church. One sees the need for expanded explanations, the heightening of miraculous elements, and even the growth of legend. Paul, who wrote his epistles between A.D. 49 and 62, simply proclaimed, "God was in Christ." It was not his intention or his need to explain how that great and mighty wonder came to pass. It was quite enough to testify to the reality of the experience of the Christian community that in Jesus of Nazareth God had been encountered, met, and worshiped. Hence, Paul proclaimed; he did not explain.

Inevitably, critics of the Christian movement began to question this assumption. How did the holy God get into this Jesus? By the time Mark wrote in A.D. 65–70, he offered an explanation. At his baptism, Mark tells us, the heavens opened, and the Spirit of God entered this Jesus, and God owned him as his unique son. That was the only written Gospel explanation the church had for about twenty years. In the middle of the eighties of the first century, two additional Gospels appeared in two different parts of the world written by two different people, neither of whom appears to have known about the other. They were Matthew and Luke. They both employed Mark, but in remarkably different ways; and they both had another common source, a collection of Jesus' sayings called *Quelle*.

By this time the weakness of the Markan explanation of the source of Jesus' divinity had become apparent. Mark alone can be read as supporting an adoptionist Christology; that is, Jesus was adopted into God at his baptism, a position clearly inadequate to the fullness of the Christian claim for their Lord. Both Matthew and Luke sought to correct that erroneous Markan impression by suggesting that his divinity was not imparted to him at baptism but at conception. He was conceived by the power of the Spirit. In his conception and birth, divinity and humanity were wondrously merged. But by the time the Fourth Gospel was written some fifteen to twenty years later, even that appeared to be an inadequate explanation. Perhaps people had already begun to literalize the birth narrative into biological rather than theological truth.

In any event, the Fourth Gospel drops the birth narratives completely and substitutes a moving and profound theological treatise we call the Johannine prologue, which says that neither baptism nor conception is an adequate explanation of how God was in Jesus. From the dawn of time, writes John, the Word was with God and the Word was God and in the Word was life which was the light of men and women. That Word was made flesh and dwelt among us. This was the Fourth Gospel's explanation of the source of the power in Jesus of Nazareth. An explanation that was not necessary for Paul had certainly become necessary as the church sought to defend and explain what Christians believed as they moved into wider and wider orbits and into more and more alien cultures. Not to embrace the chronological gap between Paul and John deprives one of helpful insights into the growth of Christian thought and Christian theology.

We also need to recognize that between us and the actual history the New Testament describes there is first of all a translation from Aramaic into Greek and then a second translation into English. Secondly and even more important, there is an oral period of at least twenty years' duration during which there were no written records at all before Paul's first epistle. Between the time of Jesus and the first Gospel, there was a thirty-five-year gap during which only an oral tradition existed. It does not take a genius to realize what happens to an oral tradition as it is passed from life to life or from community to community. The opportunity for distortion and human error is enormous.

When we seek to enter and probe that oral period we hit a dark curtain that we can penetrate only in a speculative way. What was not important in the ongoing life of the early church clearly would not be remembered or repeated. For example, the relationship of the Christians to the civil government was an everyday problem. Should Christians pay taxes or should they join a guerilla movement? Time and time again, the remembered words of Jesus would be quoted, "Render to Caesar the things that are Caesar's and to God the things that are God's." In the historic moment of fracture between the Christian movement and Judaism when Christianity found it could no longer live as a sect of Judaism, it was terribly important that *a word from the Lord* anticipating this fracture could be quoted. Indeed, the conflict could have shaped that word or even created it.

What was remembered, told, and retold in that oral period was inevitably determined and shaped by the apologetic needs of the early church. No one was being dishonest, but objectivity was again being battered. How anyone can be a biblical literalist is difficult for me to understand, for it requires one to ignore reams of data and to make completely irrational assumptions. Perhaps that is the clue. Literalism or fundamentalism is not rational. It is a religious attempt in a pseudorational form to minister to the human insecurity that craves certainty and authority. The anger that so frequently is part of threatened fundamentalists when they confront those they call *modern secularists* betrays something quite different from either certainty or love. The oft-muttered threat of hell, fire, and damnation makes sense only when viewed in this light.

When we turn these insights onto that part of the New Testament that tells the Easter story, some interesting and provocative possibilities emerge.

Lest anyone misunderstand, let me state categorically that I am convinced that there is an objective reality to Easter. Whatever Easter was, it was experienced by historic people in finite time and space and with life-changing intensity. I believe that the word *Easter* stands for and was a tremendous moment of rending truth in which the disciples experienced Jesus of Nazareth who had died to be alive again in a way that defied description and broke barriers. To me, that is the center and heart of Christianity. But it is essential to face the biblical fact that even in the Bible there is no description of the actual Moment of Resurrection. No one claims to have been an eyewitness of the Resurrection Moment. Only in the apocryphal Gospel of Peter written about A.D. 150 do we get to that level of literalism. In the New Testament, the Resurrection is neither depicted nor described. The raised Christ is the emphasis, not the moment of his being raised.

People defensive about what they believe and eager to give the *faith test* to another always seem to ask, "Do you believe in the physical resurrection of Jesus?" The question is both naïve and biblically illiterate, for the Resurrection of Jesus in the Bible is distinctly not physical *resuscitation,* which is what the question presumes. Even if one literalizes the story of the raising of Lazarus, clearly Lazarus was called back to this earthly existence from which he would at some later date have to die again. But the Resurrection of Jesus is certainly not physical in the sense that the resurrection of Lazarus was. Paul was claiming this clearly when he wrote, "Christ being raised from the dead dieth no more. Death has no more power over him." The details in the resurrection narratives of the Bible clearly do not refer to physical categories. Even the most literal reading of the New Testament portrays the risen Lord appearing and disappearing in a most nonphysical way and as entering rooms where the doors are locked and the windows are barred. These are clearly *nonphysical* symbols.

What the person posing that question is really attempting to ask is not whether Jesus' resurrection was physical, but whether or not the Easter event is real. And human language is so bound to time and space, to the limited categories of an earthbound vocabulary, that the question is quite difficult to put. If I had only the categories of physical and spiritual to describe the Moment of Easter, I would with great reluctance choose *physical* as the least limited and therefore more accurate word because *spiritual* has become an airy word that sometimes means not real, ghostly. But frankly, the word *physical* is a dreadfully inadequate word, which limits to the point of falsifying the experience that word is seeking to convey. *Physical* is simply not big enough nor broad enough to embrace the meaning of Easter.

If I had only the categories of objective and subjective to apply to the Moment of Easter, I would choose *objective* because the word *subjective* has come to mean something that is real only in the mind of a subject. But once again *objective* is not nearly a big enough word or category to grasp the meaning of Easter. The paucity of the English language becomes apparent when we try to describe that which is beyond our human experience and perception.

The best I can say is that Easter was experienced by historic people in objective history, but Easter itself is of a dimension that is greater than our ability to describe it. There are measurable effects of Easter, but Easter itself is not measurable. So we can demonstrate that something happened, but we cannot photograph or describe that which created the effects that we can demonstrate. The Easter Moment must be big enough to account for and to embrace the changes it produced, but we must get behind the limited words, the human understandings that created the written Easter tradition.

Chapter 13

A Contradictory Witness

The Christian faith was born in the Moment of Easter. Yet somewhat surprisingly that Moment is written about rather briefly in the Christian scriptures and then only in terms of the experience of the witnesses, never in terms of what Jesus experienced. One chapter out of Matthew, nine verses in Mark, one chapter in Luke, two chapters in John (one of which—chapter 21—is generally regarded as not being part of the original Johannine corpus), and a few verses in Paul represent the total content dedicated to a narration of this crucial Moment.

As brief as this is, however, the material is rich and pays dividends in insight to those who will explore it in depth. I am surprised and discouraged by how little this material is treated with seriousness in sermons from the pulpit of Christian churches. The liturgical churches observe the great forty days of Easter as a major season of the church year, but there are few churches in which the Resurrection is treated homiletically for that entire season. Even the sermon on

Easter day to the largest congregation of the year is apt to be a bit truncated. On that day the service is a bit longer, the music a bit more special, the crowd in a festive mood so that the sermon can be both brief and shallow and no one will be critical—no one except those who do not come again until the following Easter.

Certainly such treatment of this great central affirmation is not appropriate to its power. I wonder what would happen in our churches if an Easter series of sermons on the Resurrection giving some evidence of a serious exploration by the clergy were announced in advance and well advertised in the community? I suspect there would be a surprising amount of interest and excitement, for there is not a person living who is unconcerned about the issue of life's ultimate destiny. The ancient question framed by Job is still a haunting one today: "If a man (or woman) die, shall he (or she) live again?" (Job 14:14).

So now let us draw into focus the biblical record about the Easter Moment and try to push our sources back as far as we can.

Enormously enriching means of studying the Bible have been made available to scholars in the last 100 years. Form criticism, linguistic analysis, textual reconstruction and redaction, archaeological insights have all contributed to the explosion of biblical knowledge. Many from the days of William Jennings Bryan (especially in his attempts to defend the State of Tennessee against Clarence Darrow and Mr. Scopes) and many within organized religious institutions today have feared this scholarship. There has always been an element of Christianity that is anti-intellectual. Such an attitude is still present and will undoubtedly find expression in some of the reactions to this book. Most biblical scholars are never read by lay persons.

But this volume is not technical. It is written for lay people. It will attempt to popularize the commonplace insights of the scholars. It is written by a bishop who is fair game for criticism, for as one clergyman wrote me, "Bishops are supposed to defend the faith, not explore it; they are to be ritual performers, not scholars."

I am convinced that the only authentic *defense of the faith* involves honest scholarship, not anti-intellectual hiding from truth. There is a sense in which our scholarship ought to be so deep, so honest, and so intense that the result will be either that what we believe will crumble before our eyes, incapable of being sustained; or that we will discover a power and a reality so true that our commitment will be total. If we do not risk the former, we will never discover the latter. Nothing less than this seems worthy of Christians.

We turn now to some biblical facts and biblical data that I find, surprisingly enough, are not part of the conscious memory of most Christians, including most clergy. The same thing has happened to the Easter narratives of the Bible that happened to the birth narratives. They have been blended in the minds of people, and in the blending process their irreconcilable conflicts are ignored. We act as if the biblical witness is one consistent witness. Most of us have an image of the Bible as a whole, smoothed out by ignorance or a faulty memory. Few of us embrace the details of its various parts. Thus, conflicts in the biblical record are seldom faced with honesty, or some incredible, nonsensical explanation is given. I remember hearing Professor Raymond Brown, the world-famous Roman Catholic New Testament scholar, discussing the irreconcilable conflicts between Matthew's birth narrative and Luke's birth narrative. This conflict, he said, had been smoothed over by the simplistic explanation that Matthew recorded Joseph's version of the birth of Jesus and Luke recorded Mary's version. That explanation has many problems, Dr. Brown suggested, not the least of which is that "it assumes that Joseph and Mary never talked to each other."

The first thing an honest and serious probe into the truth of the Resurrection must face is the conflict and serious inconsistency that appears in the Easter narratives. Samuel Butler, in his autobiographical novel, *The Way of All Flesh,* tells us that it was precisely the discovery of these discrepancies that caused his hero, a clergyman's son (in reality Butler himself), to lose his Christian faith and to become an agnostic. The late James A. Pike, the former Episcopal Bishop of California whose strange, creative, and contraversional career is still remembered by thousands, confessed in one of his last books, *The Other Side,* that this same discovery led to his abandonment of the orthodox Christian belief in Jesus' Resurrection.

In the secularized society of our twentieth-century world, the scientific and philosophical objections to belief in the Resurrection loom large. When we add to this the publicly acknowledged fact of significant discrepancies in the Christian record of its own belief, the problem of believing with integrity becomes immense for the person who yearns to be both a part of the Christian faith and a part of his own century and world. Ignoring the data, pretending it's not there, or failing to acknowledge it is not a help. So let me bring the biblical record into clear and stark focus and relief.

There are five accounts (Professor Raymond Brown

says seven, for he subdivides Mark and John) in the New Testament that purport to give us the specific content of the Easter event. Each of the Gospels has an account, and Paul, writing to the church in Corinth, gives us his version. We will examine them in what I believe to be their chronological order, but let the reader be warned that the world of New Testament scholarship is far from unanimous in agreement on the dating of the various books of the New Testament.

There is general agreement, however, that Paul is the earliest Christian author whose writings have been preserved. So 1 Corinthians 15 is presumably the first written version of the Easter event. 1 Corinthians is generally dated A.D. 55–56, earlier than any Gospel, though perhaps not earlier than portions of the various passion narratives that come finally to lodge in the corpus of the several Gospels.

Isolating Paul's version from the Gospels, we discover the following facts: (*a*) there is in Paul's account no reference to the women's discovering the empty tomb; (*b*) there is a reference to an appearance to James alone and to "five hundred brethren at once," two accounts that are mentioned nowhere in any of the Gospels; and (*c*) Paul asserts that his own conversion experience was a resurrection appearance.

Paul's conversion is generally dated one to six years after the events of Good Friday and the first Easter. Yet Paul distinguishes his conversion experience in no way from the appearances in the other resurrection traditions except to say that his was last. "Last of all he appeared unto me." This would appear to argue that Paul agrees with John, and Mark by implication, that it is the already ascended, glorified Lord of heaven who was experienced in the resurrection appearances. It also places Paul squarely against Luke, who quite specifically states that the resurrection appearances were pre-ascension phenomena, which is one of the major unresolved conflicts in the New Testament data regarding the Easter Moment. That is the Pauline witness.

The Gospel of Mark is generally believed to be the earliest canonical Gospel and is dated by most scholars between A.D. 65 and 70. Mark's resurrection narrative is only eight verses long, and recorded in it are no resurrection appearance stories at all. Mark says that very early on the first day of the week three women (Mary Magdalene, Mary the mother of James, and Salome) came to the tomb bearing sweet spices with which they planned to anoint his body. As they walked, they wondered how they should remove the great stone that sealed the tomb's entrance. But arriving, they saw the stone removed. Entering the sepulchre, they found a young man wearing a long white garment, and the women were afraid. The young man calmed their fears, announced the Resurrection of Jesus, and invited the women to tell Peter and the disciples that he was going before them to Galilee and he would meet them there. The women departed quickly, trembling and amazed. They said nothing to anyone, for they were afraid. The Markan narrative ends quite abruptly here.

There is a lively debate in New Testament circles as to whether Mark's Gospel actually ended at this point or whether, perhaps, the original ending was torn off the scroll and lost. The weight of scholarship leans toward the conclusion that Mark intended this abrupt ending. Obviously it bothered early scribes, for they appended verses 9–21 to Mark's sixteenth chapter in an obvious attempt to harmonize Mark with the other Gospels, especially Luke. The King James Bible includes these verses in its text, but no New Testament scholar I know today regards them as original to Mark.[10] For our purposes we will regard only the first eight verses of chapter 16 as the original resurrection narrative of Mark.

Luke was aware of Mark. Indeed, in the final draft of Luke's Gospel, great sections of Mark's narrative are simply inserted into the Lukan text. There is no evidence that would suggest that Luke was aware of Matthew or that Matthew was aware of Luke. Both appeared at approximately the same time but in totally different parts of the empire. I would date both Luke and Matthew around A.D. 85–90.

In Luke's resurrection narrative some women went to the tomb. They were, however, not quite the same women as in Mark, or at least it was a larger group. Luke suggests that it was Mary Magdalene, Mary the mother of James, and Joanna, a person mentioned only one other time in the New Testament (Lk. 8:3). But he also adds the note that other women were also with them. They too went at dawn and found the stone rolled away. No explanation is given as to how it was rolled away. Entering the tomb, they confronted two men, not one, and not necessarily young as in Mark, and the long white garment that Mark described is now dazzling apparel, suggesting at the very least that these were beings of supernatural origin. The women in awe responded as if they were in the presence of the holy, and they bowed their faces to the ground. The two men gave the resurrection message, "Why do you seek the living among the dead?" The men reminded the women of Jesus' Galilean prediction of arrest, crucifixion, and resurrection. The women remembered as did Luke's original audience, who had only recently heard chapter 9 read. They returned to the disciples with the news of this encounter. The disciples, distrusting the reliability of the women's report, did not believe them.

In Luke's narrative there is no appearance of the risen Lord to the women. There is no reference to an appearance in Galilee. Contrary to Mark where we are told the women said nothing to anyone, in Luke they immediately reported to the disciples.

Luke then relates the story of an appearance by Jesus to two disciples, Cleopas and his friend, on a road to Emmaus, a village some six miles from Jerusalem. This story is mentioned nowhere else in the Bible.

The Emmaus participants returned to Jerusalem to share their news with the other disciples only to discover that Jesus had also appeared to Simon Peter, who along with the other disciples was still in Jerusalem. As the two groups talked, Jesus appeared suddenly in their midst. They ate together. Jesus commanded them to stay in Jerusalem until they received the gift of the Spirit. Then he departed. Galilee is never a setting for the Easter experience in Luke either in fact or by implication.

When we turn to Matthew, who also wrote his work in the eighties of the first century, we have other interesting and significant variations. In this narrative only two women went to the tomb at dawn on the first day of the week. They were identified by Matthew as Mary Magdalene and the other Mary. The sense of the miraculous and the supernatural has clearly been heightened. There was an earthquake. An angel of the Lord descended and rolled back the stone from the entrance to the tomb. There was no doubt that this messenger was from the heavenly realm. His face was like lightning, and his garments were white as snow. Once he had rolled the stone away, he sat upon it. His presence was so magnificent and so eerie that the guards trembled and then fainted, becoming, as Matthew suggests, "like dead men" (Mt 28:4).

The angel gave the resurrection message: "He has risen. Come see the place where he lay. Then go quickly. Tell his disciples that he has risen from the dead and he is going before you to Galilee. There you will see him" (Mt 28:6ff). The women with both fear and great joy rushed to tell the disciples. But before they arrived, Jesus himself stood in their path and greeted them. The women came up, took hold of his feet, and in obeisance worshiped him. He repeated the angel's message: "Do not be afraid; go and tell my brethren to go to Galilee, and there they will see me."

Matthew alone adds the story of the guards' reporting all that had happened to the chief priests who took counsel with the elders and bribed the guards to tell people that the disciples had stolen his body while they were asleep. Since sleeping on guard duty was a capital offense, the promise of sanctuary from persecution was also given. This story, Matthew asserts in a clearly apologetic vein, is still spread among the Jews "to this day" (Mt 28:11ff).

Then Matthew concludes his Gospel by telling of that promised Galilean rendezvous (Mt 28:16ff). It was on an unnamed Galilean mountaintop to which Jesus had directed them. When the disciples saw him, they worshiped him. He was clearly of another dimension. The implication is that this was the resurrected, ascended, glorified Lord who proclaimed, "All authority in heaven and on earth is given to me." Jesus then commissioned the disciples to "go and make disciples of all nations," baptizing them "in the name of the Father and of the Son and of the Holy Spirit," the first and only time the trinitarian formula is used in the Gospels. Jesus, the timeless Christ, also promised to be with them even "to the close of the age." On this note Matthew's Gospel ends.

Finally, there is the testimony of John. I date John around A.D. 100, but about the dating of this profound piece of writing there is more controversy than about any other New Testament book. I am personally unconvinced by arguments supporting a much earlier date given recently by both John A. T. Robinson and Raymond Brown. I do not think, however, that this is critical for our purposes in this volume. Perhaps the point at which it might make some difference is that I am convinced that the author of the Fourth Gospel was aware of and had read Mark, Luke, and Matthew, but that is not universally agreed to in the world of New Testament scholarship. More scholars would agree that the author of John knew Mark than would agree that he knew Matthew and Luke. I believe he knew all three. At the very least he seems to be in touch with much of the content of Luke's special source that scholars call "L."

John's account of the Easter Moment contains unique similarities and differences (John 20). Like the other Gospels, he starts with the women at the tomb, but now it is only one woman, Mary Magdalene. She discovered the stone rolled away and the tomb empty. There were no messengers, human or divine. There were no supernatural events, no earthquakes, no guards in a dead sleep. Mary Magdalene ran and told Peter. Peter and another disciple rushed to the tomb to verify Mary's report. Then they departed. Mary lingered. Again she looked in the tomb. This time she saw two supernatural figures that John calls angels sitting there one at the head and the other at the foot where the body had lain. Yet she was strangely unimpressed. Mary and the angels conversed, "Woman, why are you weeping?" "Because they have taken away my Lord, and I know not where they have laid him." That is hardly a resurrection message.

Then the Fourth Gospel says Mary turned around and saw Jesus standing but did not recognize him. Jesus spoke to her, "Woman, why are you weeping?"— the identical words the angels had used. Mary, supposing him to be the gardener, said to him, "Sir, if you have carried him away, tell me where you have laid him, and I will take him away." Jesus then spoke her name, "Mary." "Rabboni—teacher," she replied. Then a fascinating bit of dialogue is related. "Do not cling to me, Mary, for I have not yet ascended to the Father, but go tell my brethren that I am ascending to my Father and your Father, to my God and your God." Mary went, and to the disciples she said, "I have seen the Lord," and she relayed his messages to them.

Later that day and still in Jerusalem, the now ascended (please note) Lord appeared to the disciples. Jesus breathed on them, and they received the Holy Spirit. Both ascension and pentecost for the Fourth Gospel are events of Easter day. The commission to go forth was also, according to John, given on Easter day in Jerusalem and included the power to forgive or retain sins. From this gathering, it is noted, Thomas was absent. The disciples related this experience to Thomas, but he did not believe it. Some time passed.

On the first day of the second week, another resurrection experience occurred, according to the Fourth Gospel. The disciples were still in Jerusalem. Once more they were assembled in the upper room. It was evening, the time of the evening meal. Thomas was present. The risen Lord appeared, confronted Thomas, offered the nail prints in his hands and the wound in his side to Thomas as evidence of his identity. Thomas responded, "My Lord and my God." An editorial word is added about the virtue of believing without seeing and a closing paragraph stating that "Jesus did many other things in the presence of the disciples which this book does not include." These are written, the author states, so that the reader "may believe that Jesus is the Christ, the Son of God, and believing may have life in his name." Here the twentieth chapter ends.

It seems to many that this is where the author meant to end his work, but there is another chapter added that most scholars, including Raymond Brown, C. H. Dodd, and Rudolf Bultmann, assert is a later addendum by a different author. But who wrote it or when makes little difference for our purposes.

In chapter 21 the scene has moved from Jerusalem to Galilee. Obviously, some time had passed since the events of chapter 20. The disciples had resumed their life routines. Led by Peter, they had returned to their fishing trade, but not all of them—only Peter; the sons of Zebedee, James and John; Thomas; Nathanael; and two others who were not named. They worked through the night. As dawn broke, Jesus on the shore inquired about their catch. They did not recognize him. They responded, "We have caught no fish." Jesus instructed them to cast the net on the right side of the boat. They did so, and the catch was enormous. They could not even haul it in. The disciple identified as "the one Jesus loved" said to Peter, "It is the Lord." Peter put on his clothes and swam to the shore. The others stayed in the boat, dragging their catch the 150 yards to shore.

On land they saw a charcoal fire, fish cooking, and bread. They hauled in their net—153 fish in all. They ate breakfast. "No one," the Fourth Gospel strangely says, "dared ask him, who are you? They knew it was the Lord."

Following the sharing of this meal by the sea in Galilee, the risen Lord confronted Peter, inquiring as to his love and charging him to "feed my sheep." Finally, there is a cryptic reference to the death of Peter and the death of the beloved disciple. This is the end of the biblical description of the Easter Moment.

Something so very basic to the Christian proclamation as the Resurrection is thus the subject of great confusion and contradiction even in the writings of the Gospels, the primary written Christian witnesses. Let me summarize the points of conflict.

Who went to the tomb at dawn on the first day of the week? Paul says nothing about anyone's going. Mark says that Mary Magdalene, Mary the mother of James, and Salome went. Luke says that Mary Magdalene, the other Mary, Joanna, and some other women went. Matthew says that Mary Magdalene and the other Mary only went. John says that Mary Magdalene alone went.

What did the women find at the tomb? Since Paul has no reference to the tomb visit, his voice is silent on all the remaining details. But Mark says they found a young man in a white garment who gave the resurrection message. Luke says it was two men in dazzling apparel. Matthew says nothing less than "an angel of the Lord" who descended in an earthquake, put the armed guard to sleep, rolled back the stone, and gave the resurrection message. John begins with no messenger at all, but on Mary Magdalene's second visit, she confronted two angels, and finally confronted Jesus himself whom she mistook for the gardener until he spoke her name.

Did the women see the risen Lord in the garden at dawn on the first day of the week? No, says Mark. No, says Luke. Yes, says Matthew. Yes, but it was a little bit later, says John.

Where did the risen Christ appear to the disciples? Paul gives no hint of location in his list of appearances. Mark records no appearance stories, but he hints that there would be a meeting in Galilee. Luke says that resurrection appearances occurred only in the Jerusalem area, in the upper room, and at the village of Emmaus just six miles away. Further, Luke has the risen Lord, in clear contradistinction to Mark and Matthew, command the disciples not to leave Jerusalem until they have received the power of the Spirit. Matthew is very specific. The risen Lord appeared to the disciples only in Galilee and on top of a mountain. John says appearances of the risen Lord occurred first in Jerusalem in the upper room on two occasions separated by a week. The twenty-first chapter of John says that much later appearances did take place in Galilee, not on a mountain as Matthew states, but by a lake.

When did the risen Christ appear to the disciples? Paul says it was on the first day of the week for the first Easter experience, but he then stretches the time of resurrection appearances to include his own conversion perhaps as late as six years after the crucifixion. Mark hints that it will be at some indefinite time in the future. Luke says on the first day of the week after the crucifixion and for a period of forty days thereafter. Matthew says some days or weeks after the episode of the empty tomb when they all gathered in Galilee. John says it was on the first day of the week at evening and one week later at the same time of the day and then much later in Galilee.

Was it the resurrected but not yet ascended and glorified Lord who appeared, or was it the resurrected, ascended Lord of heaven that they experienced alive? Paul clearly implies the latter. Mark says nothing but hints that it will be the ascended, glorified Lord they will meet in Galilee. Luke argues that all resurrection appearances ceased with the ascension. As the author of Acts, he places Paul's conversion in a different category. That was a vision from heaven, not a resurrection experience as Paul claims. For Luke, it was the risen Lord who, after appearing to his disciples, ascended into heaven; and it was the ascended Lord now united with the Father who poured the Holy Spirit out on the gathered church at the day of Pentecost. Matthew implies that it was the resurrected but not yet ascended Lord who confronted the women in the garden, but that it was the ascended, glorified Lord who possesses all authority and power who met them and commissioned them on the Galilean mountaintop. John says that the resurrected Lord appeared only to Mary Magdalene ("Touch me not for I have not yet ascended."). But it was the resurrected, ascended, glorified Lord who appeared to the disciples and breathed on them, imparting the Holy Spirit, and inviting

Thomas to examine his body and touch his wounds. This is true of both the Jerusalem accounts of chapter 20 and the Galilean accounts of chapter 21.

Disagreements on basic details of the Easter narratives abound in the records of the New Testament itself. Luke[11] says that resurrection, ascension, and pentecost are separate events covering a time span of some fifty days. John says that all three were events of Easter day. And even such vital details as the place where the disciples first experienced the risen Lord and the time when this all-important moment occurred are not agreed upon by the canon of Holy Scripture. Mark and Matthew say that it took place in Galilee sometime later. Luke and John say that it took place in Jerusalem on Easter day.

This is the biblical record in stark, factual detail. It presents serious interpretive and apologetic problems with which we will attempt to deal as our exploration into the heart of Easter unfolds.

We must go deeper yet.

Chapter 14

Delving beneath Scripture

The deeper we go into the exploration of any truth, the more we discover the inadequacy of language. Language points us toward a reality that it cannot capture. Part of the great knowledge explosion in the world of science in this century is still not embraced by the language we use. So long as our minds are shackled by that language we will not be able to imagine the fullness of that truth. We still talk about *the sun's setting* or *the four corners of the earth* or *up in the sky,* though the world view that created that language has been dead for 500 years. It is inevitable that our world view shapes our language and our language informs our world view. This means that language that is literalized will always distort that which it seeks to describe. Truth, no matter how true, will be falsified as soon as it is described, understood, or captured by the words and mind set of any person or generation.

This is true even in the realm of history. Objective events obviously occur, but the moment they are described, they are no longer objective. They become rather a subjective interpretation of an objective event. There is no such thing as objective history. A marvelous book title I came across in my days of living in the South announced that the contents of the volume were *An Objective History of the Civil War from the South's Point of View.* The dominant understandings of history are always written by those who win the wars and have the power to install their points of view into the orthodox position. One can, for example, read an American version of the Mexican–American War and then read a Mexican version and wonder whether it is the same war that both accounts are describing.

It is deeply important that we understand and appreciate the relativity, the inevitable mythology, the subjectivity of all language before we begin to explore the specific language that seeks to describe the Moment that gave rise to Christianity. For, I reiterate, I am convinced that there is a literalness about the truth of Easter, even though I am also convinced that the words that seek to proclaim or relay that truth cannot and should not themselves be literalized.

We have examined in some detail the conflicting testimony in the Gospel narratives in regard to the way each Gospel writer seems to understand the Easter Moment. At the very least, an open and honest facing of the irreconcilable conflict in the details of these narratives should make us ask those whose need for religious security seems to demand a biblical literalism to tell us, please, which version they want to be literal about. Conflicting accounts simply cannot be literalized without unacceptable mental gymnastics or partial blindness. But now that we have cracked open a view of the truth beyond literalism and begun to explore that vast terrain, I would like to invite the reader even deeper into the resurrection narrative.

First, we need to probe the texts for illustrations of heightened exaggeration as we attempt to get as close as we can to the primary moment in the earliest verbal description of Easter. Some textual exaggerations are easy to identify, especially if we remember that between Paul's account and the Fourth Gospel's account a period of some fifty years seems to have elapsed. Given the considerably shorter life expectancy of that era of history, fifty years meant an enormous time span of almost three generations.

In Mark's Gospel (A.D. 65–70) recall that the resurrection announcement was made by a young man. His supernatural origin is hinted at, but it is certainly not stated. By the time Matthew wrote (A.D. 85–90), all hesitancy and doubt about the supernatural original of the proclaimer of the Resurrection had been removed. It was clearly an angel who was not of this world. In Luke (A.D. 85–90) the messenger had become two supernatural angels, and one could argue that by the time of the Fourth Gospel it was no less than Jesus himself who announced the Resurrection to Mary Magdalene in the garden. There is a heightening and an exaggerating of the supernatural that is clearly at work in this small detail. Surely the enormity of the Easter message had the power to enlarge the character of the one who first announced this message.

Again in Mark the story of the women coming to the tomb at the dawn of Easter day involved a stated concern. How will they gain access to the tomb, for we have been told a massive stone has sealed the entry. However, Mark says that when the women arrived, the stone had been removed. How that happened did not seem to bother Mark at all. But details that cry out for explanation are not normally left unexplained; and where facts are unknown, imaginations prove more than equal to the task. So by the time Matthew's Gospel was written, this mystery was dramatically cleared up. In intimate detail Matthew relates that there was an earthquake and an angel descended (heaven was clearly up). The dazzling appearance blinded the group of soldiers guarding the tomb so that they appeared as dead men, and the angel rolled back the stone. Clearly in the twenty or so years between Mark and Matthew, a heightening of the account had been accomplished.

The details that surround the account of the burial are a bit more obscure, but once again we can show the probability of a developing legend. Paul, writing to the Corinthians around the year A.D. 55, states very simply, "He was buried." No details are given, no story is related, no legend is building. In the book of Acts, however, in a speech attributed to Paul it is stated that Jesus was buried by the same parties who crucified him. This unceremonial burial at the hands of his enemies was the final insult given Jesus. This story, which only Acts records, rings true when we study the burial records in regard to people who have been executed and when we remember the unquestioned tradition that the early church would not have created, namely, that after Jesus' arrest he was abandoned by his disciples. They forsook him and fled with only a few watching helplessly from afar. With their lives so filled with the constant fear that Jesus' fate awaited them if they were caught, it is reasonable to suppose that they did not step forward, claim the body, and provide a decent burial. Yet by the time the Gospels were written, that apostolic desertion was a scandal to the early church.

One of the ways they eased that pain and embarrassment was to suggest that the burial was accomplished at the hands of loving and secret disciples; hence, a legendary burial tradition arose, which suggested that one named Joseph of Arimathea performed this burial act *for* the disciples and, further, that it was performed not out of hostility but out of charity. In this manner the reputation of the disciples was partially rehabilitated.

Some scholars speculate that Joseph was, in fact, a member of the Sanhedrin who was assigned charge of the disposal of the body. This would be a customary and routine assignment in a capital case. Perhaps he handled that assignment in a sensitive way and thus won the appreciation of the mourners. In this supposed fact and custom may lie the historic kernel of truth behind the burial story. By the time of Mark's writing, however, Joseph of Arimathea was portrayed as "a respected member of the Council who was looking for the kingdom of God" (Mk. 15:43). Mark had him provide not the hasty public burial of a convicted criminal, which was Jesus' likely fate, but a carefully carried out burial usually reserved for those who died normal and respectable deaths.

By the time Luke wrote, Joseph of Arimathea had been Hellenized into "a good and righteous man" (Lk. 23:50), while in Matthew he was called "a disciple" (Mt. 27:57). The Fourth Gospel completed the Christian transformation of this shadowy figure by calling him "a secret believer" (Jn. 19:38). Again, simply by looking at the biblical stories chronologically, we can see the heightening of details, the building of a legendary tradition. It is not a quantum leap from the Joseph of Arimathea in the Gospel narrative to the tradition of Joseph's planting the dogwood tree that sprouted from his walking staff in England or the favorite children's Easter anthem entitled "In Joseph's Lovely Garden."

All of this leads to an increasing consensus about many details in the biblical tradition. For when scholars turn their spotlights on the Easter narratives, utilizing all the tools of their profession, one rule of thumb becomes apparent: the later the resurrection tradition, the more graphic, the more miraculous become the details that tradition includes. The later the narrative, the more vivid, the more detailed, the more specific the accounts become.

Paul gives us lists but no narrative details. Mark gives us a picture of an empty tomb and a proclamation of resurrection. They are the two earliest biblical writers. But the later Gospels go into all sorts of proofs buttressed by details that border on portraying the Resurrection in physical–historic reality. They touched him. He ate with them. He walked with them. He conversed with them. He charged them. But it is precisely in these details that the biblical data is most often in conflict. In these accounts we confront highly subjective matter; these vary dramatically, depending most importantly on the person relating the data.

The late Norman Perrin, former New Testament professor at the University of Chicago, outlined the theological point of view of Matthew, Mark, and Luke and then demonstrated conclusively that their narration of the Easter Moment fitted perfectly into each of their subjective theological perspectives. More than that, each Gospel asserted in its own way that the Resurrection of Jesus was a unique moment, not like any moment in the past, present, or future where someone in some sense was restored to life.

Jesus' resurrected reality was not questioned, but the risen Christ was always seen as being of a new order of reality. The risen Christ was both radically different from and continuous with the historic Jesus. He was vastly different and yet recognizable. The disciples with their human language and human vocabulary gasped at their inability to describe what they did not for a moment doubt that they were experiencing. Paul was driven to coin the term *spiritual body* to capture this reality. At the very least we become aware that the truth of Easter is not and cannot be captured by words. To find the truth of the Easter Moment, we must go behind or beneath the words used to convey the power of Easter.

A second vital detail emerges when we press our data in a slightly different but clearly related direction. When all the biblical texts purporting to describe the Easter event are scrutinized, it becomes apparent that the risen Lord was not just seen by anyone or everyone. There is clearly a subjective dimension to the experience of resurrection. The only eyes that *saw* the risen Lord were eyes that had in some sense become believing eyes. Pilate, Caiaphas, Annas, the soldiers, the crowd of uncommitted spectators—none of these had resurrection experiences. They were not called out of unbelief into faith.

I suppose that those who are prone to literalism could argue that Thomas fits this category, but even on a literal basis Thomas was much more like Peter than Pilate. He was a member of the believing community. He fell away and was recalled. His recalling took a primary, not a secondary, experience, causing the author of the Fourth Gospel to chastise him a bit by saying, "Blessed are those who do not see and yet who believe." But the Fourth Gospel is clear that Thomas never abandoned the community of faith even when he was the only unconvinced member, so he could hardly be called an objective or hostile witness.

A second observation emerges in that even the believers are portrayed as being in the presence of the risen Lord, but they were unable to see him as *resurrected* until *their eyes were opened*. This motif is present in the Emmaus Road story (Lk. 24:13ff), in the appearance by the Sea of Galilee in John (Jn. 21:4ff), and in Mary Magdalene's mistaking of him for the gardener (Jn. 20:11ff).

Beneath this strange detail which survives, though it does not flatter the early disciples, is another insight that sheds light on the Easter Moment. The biblical writers seem to be saying that there was a powerful and necessary element of subjectivity in the resurrection drama. That is, the subjects who experienced the Easter Moment were first of all related to this Jesus, and secondly something seemed to happen to them that *opened their eyes* and enabled them to see. The risen Lord does not appear to be objective in the sense that he could walk down a Jerusalem street and be greeted by casual passers-by.

This fact indicates to me that our human categories of subjective and objective are woefully inadequate to use in regard to the Easter Moment. Subjective tends to mean something that is true only in the mind of a subject. Surely the Easter Moment could not be reduced to that. But objective tends to mean physical, photographable, and measurable. That category appears to be equally inadequate to capture the essence of Easter. Both categories, even when stretched to their limits, appear inadequate. The Moment of Easter appears to be subjective at some points, objective at others, but essentially it is always beyond both categories. We have the apparently physical details in the Easter narratives of the risen Lord's touching, eating, and seeing. But side by side and never blocked out by physical, objective rhetoric are the nonphysical details of appearing and reappearing, of entering a room where doors were locked and windows were barred.

Whatever the Easter Moment was, it appears to be beyond the skills of the scientist to measure, beyond the categories of the historian to demonstrate. Every description is inevitably a distortion, but that distortion does not mean that the event being described was not real. Easter was a new reality breaking into the consciousness of the old reality and revealing the woeful inadequacy of limited minds and limited words to describe the inbreaking reality. We are on the razor's edge of human rationality.

Armed with this insight, we once more read the resurrection accounts of the New Testament, and another suggestion crystallizes. The first Gospel written, Mark, contains no narrations of resurrection appearances at all. The earliest New Testament account of the Resurrection is from Paul. It contains lists of those who saw the risen Christ but again not one single narrative detail. When one sees how contradictory the narrative details are in the later Gospels, one has to suspect that the content of all the appearance stories was not a part of the original Moment of Easter. Narrative descriptions of the details of resurrection appearances all seem to be later creations of the believing community. Many of these details have clear homiletic and apologetic motifs.

This is an idea that appeals to me more and more the deeper I go into this study, for there is a radical primacy about Easter in the New Testament. There is not one verse of the New Testament that does not assume the reality of Easter. Yet in the narrative of the Moment of Easter or the details of Easter, there is an unsettling and confusing sea of contradictions. Furthermore, these contradictions were allowed to remain side by side in the sacred scripture, and except for the later addition to Mark (16:9–21) and perhaps the twenty-first chapter of John, no attempt to harmonize these accounts was undertaken. These facts would argue to me that inside the community of faith there never was a literal reading of the Easter narratives. There was rather from the very beginning a tacit understanding that the reality of the Easter Moment was beyond what human words could capture or human pictures could envision. Yet we needed words and pictures, and so the Easter Moment in time created both; but neither the narrative words nor the pictorial explanation was original to Easter.

Originally, the Easter Moment (the Resurrection) seems to me to have been simply proclaimed, not narrated. The earliest Christians were content to proclaim, for they had touched a truth and perceived a realm beyond the capacity of words to describe or narratives to explain. They did not for a moment doubt its truth. Certainly there is good reason to believe that the confidence of the participants in the Easter Moment did not rest on anything so humanly fragile as objective historic data. They knew that death could not contain him, so they proclaimed, "He is not here." That was far more powerful and persuasive than all the narrations concerning the empty tomb. Men and women could and would forever argue about the meaning of the empty tomb.

Such arguments did rage. One version of that argument found its way into Matthew's Gospel (Mt 28:13). It suggested that the tomb was empty because the disciples had come by night and had stolen his body so that they could make the resurrection claim. This, according to Matthew, was currently held in certain Jewish circles at the time of his writing. Such a possibility could, of course, account for the emptiness of the tomb, but who in the biblical narrative was ever converted by the emptiness of the tomb? Only *that disciple whom Jesus loved* is portrayed as *believing* on the basis of the Fourth Gospel's very late and highly stylized narrative version of the empty tomb (Jn. 20:8). And the author's very obvious desire to elevate *the beloved disciple,* as he comes to be called, gives him an apologetic motive for that detail.

Countering the argument that the disciples stole the body is the vast array of impressive data that we have already developed. It must have been a tremendous startling power that embraced the disciple band, converting Peter, turning cowards hiding out in a locked and barred upper room into heroic, courageous people who braved the wrath and the persecution of the authorities to bear witness to the Resurrection. If they indeed had created a deception by stealing the body of Jesus and inventing a tale called the Resurrection to cover their act, would they have been willing to be abused, beaten, imprisoned, and martyred for a fraud?

There was another version of the argument that the literalizing of the story of the empty tomb created. Perhaps it was not the disciples but the Jewish authorities who stole the body. At least this version did not accuse the disciples of the irrational behavior of having their lives dramatically changed by their chicanery, complicated by their willingness to believe their own propaganda. This argument had a far more sophisticated and believable motive. The Jewish authorities, having been deeply troubled by the Jesus movement, wanted to make sure that the execution of Jesus in fact killed the movement. Sometimes martyrs fuel a movement rather than terminate it. Their burial places become holy shrines to which countless pilgrims journey, and in the death of the leader the movement grows stronger than it ever was in his life. One has only to remember St. Thomas à Becket and Canterbury Cathedral, for example. One way to destroy that is to destroy the body and render unknown its final resting place. Some suggested that this is what lay behind the empty tomb tradition. The disciples misunderstood and in their grief and hysteria created the legend of the Resurrection.

This argument was countered by asking questions based on the history of the early church. Christianity burst on the scene with power and impact fueled almost exclusively by the claim of resurrection. The response of the Jewish authorities was immediately to move to quell or to persecute the Christians. The Gospel words that purport to be Jesus' warnings—"You will be beaten in the synagogues (Mk. 13:9) and thrown into prison" and "Blessed are you when men hate you and when they exclude and revile you" (Lk. 6:22)—were not, in fact, predictions of events to come by an all-knowing Lord, but rather historically accurate descriptions of what did, in fact, happen.

Saul of Tarsus was undoubtedly an arm of the early

persecution of the church, and his conversion is placed by many within one year after the events of Easter. I know of no one who dates it later than six years after Easter. The martyrdom of Stephen is thought to be an actual historic moment. James, the son of Zebedee, was killed around A.D. 44. The point is that tension and persecution were early phenomena for Christians. Surely the Jewish authorities would not have been moved to physical persecution to stamp out a movement if they knew that this movement was, in fact, based upon their own destruction or removal of the physical remains of this Jesus. They could summarily have dismissed and destroyed the fledgling church by admitting their duplicity in this act. They did not. According to Matthew, they admitted the emptiness of the tomb and offered another explanation. Surely they would not have been so threatened as to move to persecution while knowing all along that the tale of the Resurrection of this Jesus was, in fact, based on a Christian misunderstanding of their own action. And so this argument raged.

There was a third empty tomb debate that found expression in the early church but which appeared in increasingly sophisticated forms in Christian history, reaching its zenith in the writing of a liberal Protestant New Testament scholar, Kirsopp Lake, at the turn of this century. This argument rested not on the culpability of either the disciples or the Jewish authorities but upon the ignorance and superstition of the women. According to this point of view, the women, who were not educated and stereotypically assumed to be emotional and given to hysteria, came to the eerie tombs at the crack of dawn. Walking in a burial ground before dawn is not a confidence-building experience even today. Our Halloween "liturgies" are filled with skeletons, ghosts, and the historic sounds of death. Fraternity initiations still place pledges in cemeteries for overnight rendezvous. So these women had their fears highly exacerbated by that setting and were not thinking clearly. When they came to the grave that they thought was the proper place, they were scared out of their wits by the gardener. The gardener tried to explain that they were at the wrong tomb. "He is not here! Behold the place where they laid him," he said pointing to another site. The women, however, misunderstood, and in the telling and retelling of this account the gardener became an angel and, in the Fourth Gospel, Jesus himself. Since the gardener was at an open and empty tomb, the legend about how the stone was rolled away from the mouth of the grave was told to account for the fact that it was unsealed. Since no one had yet been buried in that new gravesite, the grave was obviously empty. The women, as Mark suggests, fled in fear, and this is the origin of the tradition of the empty tomb.

This relatively modern reconstruction hypothesis fails to take into account one major and determinative detail, those who would counter it suggest; namely, that the status of women was so low in the first century that no one would base anything on the report of women. Women were considered only slightly more valuable than chattel. Their opinions were certainly not sought or heeded. Echoes of this attitude permeate the Easter narratives.

The women, says St. Luke, reported their experience to the disciples and "they did not believe it, for it seemed to them an idle tale" (Lk. 24:11). In the Fourth Gospel two of the disciples, Peter and *the disciple whom*

Jesus loved, sped to the tomb to investigate, for the word of the women would simply not suffice. It is a fact that the women were free to go to the tomb because they were considered too insignificant to arrest. It is also a fact that the testimony of a woman was not allowed before any tribunal in the first century.

As soon as the proclamation "He is not here" was articulated, which developed out of the conviction that death could not contain this Jesus, it was inevitable that narratives designed to give content to that faith proclamation would develop. The stories about the empty tomb represent those narrations; and as soon as narrative details are given, debate on those details and counter-explanations develop. The details are elaborated by the debate, and pro and con arguments rage. All three of the aforementioned versions have had their day in various forms. Narrative details are always debatable, but underneath those details is an undoubted proclamation that seems to me to have been the first layer of the church's Easter message: He is not here; death cannot contain him.

Finally, I think that it is important to register the fact that discovering an empty tomb would not have suggested resurrection to any of the disciples. Only a post-Easter reading back into the text would suggest that the disciples could have leaped from empty tomb to resurrection. An empty tomb would have meant only that someone had tampered with the body. It would have been a final insult, a hostile act. Their enemies were not content to destroy his life; now they have desecrated his body. It would only have heightened fear, not created faith. So we journey beyond the narrative of the empty tomb and its somewhat silly historic debate 'and arrive at a proclamation, "He is not here."

There was, however, another proclamation: "He is risen" and "We have seen the Lord." Behind all the narratives of Easter there is a conviction that this Jesus who had died has been experienced alive again. When this proclamation and conviction was narrated, it would inevitably create appearance stories. These appearance stories would also be debated, and alternative explanations would be offered. In the apologetic task of defending the authenticity of the appearances against attack, apologetic details would undoubtedly be added to the narratives. When critics would suggest that it must have been a vision or that their minds were playing tricks on them, the Christians would respond by talking of seeing the nail prints in his hands and his feet, of eating with him, of having the risen Lord say, "Touch me. Does a ghost have flesh as I have?" (Lk. 24:39–40).

The narrative details of the appearance stories have also been vigorously debated and defended throughout Christian history. Alternative explanations have been offered and from the Christian perspective demolished or rendered absurd. In the course of history these alternative explanations have been variations of three major themes.

First, there was the suggestion that the disciples had a vision of Jesus alive in the bosom of Abraham and that this was exaggerated into resurrection stories. I do not want to debate the possibility of visions at this point. I only comment that history more than once has turned on what someone has called a vision. I think of Constantine on the eve of the Battle of Milvian Bridge seeing a cross in the sky and the inscription, "In this sign conquer," or of Joan of Arc's visions which fueled her forces for their battles against Britain. People have believed themselves to have had visions, and these visions have determined the shape of their lives. Could the Easter experience have been of the same genre?

Countering this suggestion has been the argument that we can presume that Jesus and his disciples already believed in life after death. Certainly Jesus' arguments with the Sadducees about whose wife the widow of the seven brothers will be in the kingdom of heaven would indicate that (Mt. 22:25ff.). Jesus also interpreted the Old Testament's statements where God referred to himself as the God of Abraham, Isaac, and Jacob to mean that these three ancient patriarchs were not dead but living (Mt. 22:32ff.). In the parable of Lazarus and Dives recorded only by Luke, there is a clear reference to both an abode of bliss in the bosom of Abraham and an abode of torment in the nethermost regions of Sheol. In the story of the raising of Lazarus (Lk. 16:20ff.), Lazarus' sister Martha said, "Lord, I know he will live again at the general resurrection of the last day." Since Jesus and presumably his disciples already believed in life after death, why would a vision of Jesus alive do anything more than confirm what they already believed? Why would that create such dramatic changes, such galvanized activity? Confirmation of already-believed data hardly has life-changing power.

Beyond that, though it is not my purpose to seek to do an exhaustive exegesis of the account of the transfiguration story, I think it ought at the very least to be noted that this episode purports to be a vision of people who were dead, namely, Moses and Elijah, now seen to be alive (Mk. 9:4 ff.). That vision did not seem to open the eyes of understanding for the disciples, and it certainly did not energize or redirect their lives.

They wanted to stay on the mountain in the first place, and when they did descend, they discovered themselves to be both inept and powerless. Hence, it is argued that visions (subjective visions of Jesus alive) simply cannot adequately account for the Easter phenomenon.[12]

Perhaps the disciples hallucinated, others suggested. Perhaps vision is too subjective a word or too rational a concept. It was a highly emotional time. The trauma was intense. Their master had been taken from them, tried, beaten, tortured, mocked, and executed. In a moment they had become fugitives. Perhaps their emotional systems created hallucinatory shock absorbers to calm their fears, absolve their guilt, and minimize their trauma and grief. Hence, through hallucinatory encounters they became convinced that Jesus was alive and objectively in their midst; and they could touch him, converse with him, and eat with him. This would galvanize the disciples, reorient their lives, and empower them to live, to suffer, to die without fear. No duplicity would be involved, for hallucinating people are convinced of the authenticity of their hallucinations. Could the appearances of the risen Lord be understood in this fashion? With many variations this alternative explanation to the narrative accounts of the appearances has been offered through the centuries.

Christians have countered this by suggesting that such an explanation assumes that the same hallucinatory content could have informed so many people's experiences (I Cor 15). Paul in the earliest account of the Resurrection lists those who had seen the risen Lord. This list includes Peter and the disciples, James, and the apostles, and 500 brethren at once. Professor Reginald Fuller goes to great lengths to demonstrate that the disciples and the apostles were two different groups.* He also suggests that this list was part of the earliest tradition of the Christian Church. Paul is clearly passing on what he has received. He adds to it the note that he too was the recipient of a resurrection experience, and clearly he did not share in the trauma and grief that supposedly produced the emotional state that induced hallucinatory behavior.

The total New Testament portrayal of the disciples certainly does not present us with subjects that seem by any other measures likely to be given to hallucinations. They responded to Jesus' arrest in a cowardly, but quite rational, way. They fled for their lives. Following his death, at least according to Luke, they went into hiding, being careful to secure the doors and windows. And last but not least, the Easter narratives of the New Testament do not portray men possessing hallucinatory certainty, but rather human beings responding to Easter in a completely rational and highly skeptical way. To doubt the Resurrection was hardly flattering to the disciples when the New Testament was written, and yet references to their incredulity in the face of the Easter experience are deeply rooted in the New Testament. The Thomas story in the Fourth Gospel elevates the skepticism to the major motif of that particular narration.

A relatively modern version of the hallucinatory suggestion as an explanation for the appearance phenomenon connected with the Easter narration is the suggestion that the disciple band and Jesus himself were on some drug or weed, some ancient version of LSD. It is an ingenious new version of the ancient

*The Formation of the Resurrection Narratives, p. 27 ff.

argument. It must be noted that the arguments against the truth of the Resurrection are all attempts to give alternate explanations to the narrations of Easter appearances. Indeed, the narrations themselves create the counterattacks for the nonbelievers even as the contradictory details create doubt and confusion among believers.

There is a third explanation periodically offered to dispel the stories of resurrection. It, too, is ingenious and most recently was dusted off and reoffered in an imaginative and highly readable book by Hugh J. Schonfield entitled *The Passover Plot*. Basically it suggests that Jesus did not really die, that he only appeared to die, that he was in fact drugged when the sponge was given to him after he complained of thirst. Schonfield is wondrously innovative in his story. He tells of undercover residents of Jerusalem who had secret signals and passwords who also arranged for the Palm Sunday donkey and the Maundy Thursday upper room. He relates stories of duplicity among the temple guard and among those responsible for burial. They removed Jesus from the cross before death, he suggests, and in the coolness of the tomb revived him, and he was seen alive again; and this created the tales of the Resurrection.

I loved reading *The Passover Plot* because never has a thrilling mystery story been so ingeniously solved on so little data and such wild suppositions but with such exciting writing. At its core this book and all the other versions of this argument ask us to believe that one crucified could not only survive that ordeal but could also convince his followers that he had returned from the dead and was, in fact, victorious over death. Obviously, those who suggest this possibility have never been crucified. A battered, broken, bleeding, crucified victim who somehow managed to escape death in that ordeal would hardly inspire his associates to believe that he had conquered death, that in Paul's words "death has no more dominion over him." One who survived crucifixion might be considered lucky, but no one would suggest that he had escaped death forever. First-century men and women were naïve about much of the technological data of our generation, but they were not naïve about death and life, suffering and hope. To suggest that they were is foolishness on our part.

Resurrection narratives inevitably create counter-explanations. As soon as the Moment of Easter moves beyond proclamation into narrations, arguments stir, and details vary. "Jesus lives!" the disciples asserted because of their experience of Easter. "We have seen the Lord," they claimed. Then stories that narrated what had been proclaimed appeared. Just as the proclamation "He is not here" gave rise to the narrative details of the empty tomb, so the proclamation "He is risen" gave rise to the narrative accounts of the various appearance stories.

But suppose none of the narratives are part of the original Moment of Easter. Suppose that the Moment of Easter was of a dimension where words fail and language proves inadequate. Suppose that all they could do was to proclaim "death cannot contain him—he lives." Suppose that behind that proclamation lay a certainty, a conviction that was beyond the possibility of narration. Suppose the Easter Moment was beyond history in a realm called metahistory, but experienced in time by historic people so that human words had to be employed to describe what they could not ever be expected to describe. If that is so, then it is not only inevitable but clearly to be expected that attempts to narrate what can only be ecstatically proclaimed will bring conflict, confusion, misunderstanding, argument, and alternative explanations. Yet inside the experience, the conflicting narratives will be allowed to exist side by side in the biblical record and never disturb those who know its truth is deeper than the accounts of that truth. Such has been the case, I would argue, and this is why the power of the Resurrection leaped from faith to faith, from generation to generation. The proclamation, "He is not dead," may have given rise to the negative witness of the empty tomb, and "Jesus lives; we have seen the Lord" may have been the basis for the stories of Jesus' appearances. But the *truth* of Easter has never rested on anything so fragile as a consistent narration of details or objective historic data.

One final enigmatic note. In the Greek language there are two words that are translated as "body." One word is *sarx*, which is translated as "flesh" in the literal, physical sense. The other word is *soma*, which can be used as a synonym for the whole person. It is interesting to note that when Paul talks about the resurrection of the body (1 Cor. 15) he always uses *soma*, never *sarx*.

Every narrative detail beyond the simple proclamation seems to be a necessary later development, a later embellishment or explanation or defense of the theme and reality of Easter. To step behind the narration to the proclamation is not to answer all the questions, but it is to get beneath the conflict of details. It is, I am confident, to take one giant step nearer that Moment when Christianity was born. It is also to raise faith anxieties that not everyone seems able to manage. They could not manage simple proclamation in the first century, and so they moved into narration. Many whose faith is tied to the narrations cannot manage today, for to challenge or to move behind the narration for them is to move out of faith into doubt, out of certainty into fear. But we must take this step if Easter is to have integrity or theological honesty.

One cannot stop here either. We have really only begun our probe.

Chapter 15

Further Clues: The Primacy of Peter and the Third Day

As we press beyond the narrations, we have to find clues, vital details that hint at a more original insight than their present form would substantiate. In this chapter we seek to examine two such details: the role of Peter and the meaning of the third day.

We have in an earlier chapter attempted to measure the impact of the Easter Moment on Peter. Now it is important in the development of this study to reconstruct the impact of Peter upon the Easter Moment. That is not just a rhetorical trick but rather a genuine and real concern, because time and again the resurrection narratives seem to attest that in the unfolding of the resurrection drama there was a primacy for Peter.

It is attested first by Paul, who in relating the list of appearances given to him asserts, "He (Jesus) appeared first to Peter, then to the disciples." Mark has the young man at the tomb say to the women, "Go tell the disciples *and Peter* that he goes before you into

Galilee." Luke relates the story of the two men from Emmaus rushing back to Jerusalem to share with the disciples their experience of talking with the risen Lord and sharing a meal with him only to be told by the disciples that "the Lord has risen *and appeared to Peter.*"

The twentieth chapter of St. John tells us that Mary Magdalene upon the discovery of the empty tomb "ran and went *to Simon Peter* and the other disciple" and related the news. The Evangelist then tells us how Peter and the other disciple ran to the tomb; the other disciple outran Peter and came first to the sepulcher, but hesitated there and did not enter. Then Simon Peter arrived, and he was first to go into the empty tomb. Continuing into the twenty-first chapter, we see that the author of the Fourth Gospel or the author of this addendum chapter took great pains to relate in graphic detail the confrontation between the risen Lord *and Peter.* "Simon, do you love me? Feed my sheep," echoes three times as if it were a formula in a familiar liturgy.

Some biblical scholars suggest that Matthew's addition to Mark's story of Peter's confession at Caesarea Philippi was, in fact, a misplaced resurrection narrative. Jesus, recall, had asked the disciples, "Who do men say that I am?" They had replied with all of the popular suggestions: John the Baptist returned to life, Elijah, Jeremiah, one of the other prophets of old, etc. Then Jesus made the question personal and existential, "But who do you say that I am?" And Peter blurted out, "You are the Christ, the son of the Living God." Matthew's Gospel then adds, "You are Peter, and on this rock I will build my church, and the powers of death shall not prevail against it. I will give you the keys of the kingdom, and whatever you bind on earth will be bound in heaven, and whatever you loose on earth shall be loosed in heaven." There is no doubt that such a passage was a powerful witness to the primacy of Peter.

One final text may well also bear eloquent testimony to Peter's primary role in the Moment of Easter. It is written in the passion narrative of Luke. The scene is the last supper in the upper room. Jesus spoke to Peter, "Simon, Simon, behold Satan demanded to have you that he might sift you like wheat, but I have prayed for you that your faith may not fail; and *when you have turned again, strengthen your brethren.*" When that verse is read from a post-resurrection perspective, it echoes with deeper and deeper possibilities.

There is no doubt that Peter was the leader of the early church. The book of Acts makes that abundantly clear. Paul's conflict with Peter, which he relates in the Epistle to the Galatians, was an even earlier firsthand witness. The historic question is: did Peter's primacy in the early church cause those who related the narratives of Easter to cast Peter in the primary role, or do we have preserved here a peculiar witness and dramatic hint that in some way Peter was the crucial person, the primary witness in whatever the Easter Moment was? At the very least the early church was asserting that the Easter Moment had a primary witness who could be interviewed. That is, in whatever realm of truth the Resurrection was, it was perceived or experienced in history by a specific human life. In any reconstruction of the Easter Moment, the primacy of the witness of Peter must, I am convinced, be taken into account.

To press into the second clue that might help us unlock the meaning of the Easter tradition, there is a consistent New Testament reference to a dating of the

Easter Moment. It was the first day of the week or the third day after the crucifixion. The precise phrase, "on the third day," as the dating of Easter is attested by Paul, Mark, Matthew, Luke, and John. The meaning of this phrase has been thoroughly debated in the world of New Testament scholarship. Is this a chronological reference? Those who see resurrection outside of an historic reality are troubled, I believe, by an historic dating process. Yet someone in history at a particular time had to be convinced of the reality of Jesus resurrected regardless of the historicity of the content of that resurrection. The particular time when that reality broke upon the conscious mind of that historic person might well have been the third day. Hence, the references to that date might be quite literal. But if those references are not literal, from where would this universal dating assumption have arisen?

Some point to a reference in Hosea (6:2) which says, "After two days he will revive us; on the third day he will raise us up," but there is no evidence that this verse shaped the resurrection tradition. There is the analogy in the book of Jonah (1:17) that states that Jonah was in the belly of the great fish for three days and three nights. This analogy was used by Matthew (12:40) as his apologetic explanation of Jesus' being a sign like the sign of the prophet Jonah. "An evil and adulterous generation seeks for a sign, but no sign shall be given to it except the sign of the prophet Jonah. For as Jonah was three days and three nights in the belly of the whale, so will the Son of Man be three days and three nights in the heart of the earth" (Mt. 12:40). This is hardly determinative, for this verse is typical of Matthew's country preacher proof text routine; and as with so many of Matthew's proof texts, this one literally does not fit. No one who would count the time from sundown on Good Friday until dawn on Easter Sunday could possibly get three days and three nights. The time was literally thirty-six hours. Two nights and one day is the maximum one can arrive at even in Matthew's version of the Easter event. So this Jonah text is neither illuminating nor particularly applicable.

There was a popular idea in Judaism that decomposition did not begin until the fourth day after death. Some Jewish tradition added to this the idea that the spirit of the deceased hovered around the body until the third day before departing, and the spirit's departure marked the beginning of decomposition. This idea finds its way into the Fourth Gospel in the raising of Lazarus story (Jn. 11:1–53). When Jesus arrived, the Evangelist notes that Lazarus had already been dead four days. When Jesus ordered the stone removed from the tomb, Martha objected, "Lord, by this time there will be an odor, for he has been dead four days." Doubtless the writer of this Gospel saw this detail as heightening the drama and the power of this miraculous event, but in the process he captured part of the folk wisdom of his day. How much that folk wisdom shaped the tradition of *the third day* is a subject about which we can only speculate.

Professor Reginald Fuller has suggested another possibility for which he credits Maurice Goguel; but until Fuller's suggestion, Goguel's point had not been taken as very significant. In trying to recreate the first-century Jewish mind set that inevitably filtered and interpreted whatever it was that the disciples experienced on Easter, Goguel notes "several Talmudic texts where the idea occurs that the general resurrection (at the end of history) will occur three days after the end of the world."[13] These texts go on to suggest that the morning of the third day is the critical moment. It is highly possible that this understanding shaped the accounts of the Easter Moment from the very beginning.

I would like to suggest that many of these hypotheses are not mutually exclusive. We have already noted (Chapter 8) the impact of the new holy day (the first day of the week) upon the disciples. We have noted that this was so firmly entrenched in Christian tradition that by A.D. 56 Paul could refer to it without any further explanation (1 Cor. 16:2). We have sought to show that the Johannine phrase, "after eight days," in his relating of the second resurrection appearance to the disciples suggests that in John's mind the Easter Moment from the very beginning marked the first day of the week as a unique day for Christian worship. Could it be that there was a Moment on the first day of the week following the crucifixion that defied explanation and that this Moment did come to be understood in terms of the idea of the general resurrection on the third day after the end of time? Can we not at least suggest that here we have a both/and and not an either/or?

I am convinced that the Resurrection of our Lord was real, but I am not certain that history per se can contain this reality. Perhaps it was a metahistoric truth but perceived by people who lived in history, and these people must of necessity have perceived it at a particular moment of history. Hence, the primacy of Peter's witness was tenaciously held onto as a way of saying, "The truth of Easter had a primary historic witness who can be interviewed." Similarly, the universal agreement on *the third day* was a specific attempt to say that at a particular time the truth of Jesus' Resurrection, a truth that is beyond history, was perceived in history in a mind-bending, vision-heightening moment. In that Moment time-limited people experienced time-lessness, or in the words of Paul Tillich "the eternal now," and finite human life was embraced by an infinity that they could only see in terms of Jesus.

We separate these two clues from the narrative and hold them while we explore for others. Perhaps in time some of these pieces will begin to fit together.

Chapter 16

The Apocalyptic Mind

It is important to note that the earliest references to the Resurrection place the initiative with God. "Christ has been raised," says Paul (1 Cor. 15:20). "Whom God raised from the dead," says Peter in one of the sermons of Acts (Acts 3:15). Even the Greek word used for the appearances (*ophethe*) is the word used in the Septuagint to refer to angels and theophanies where the revelatory initiative lies with the angel or with God who desires to make God manifest. The experience of the recipient is clearly not primary; the action of God is. How the recipient sees in all biblical theophanies is left unclear. A marvelous story is told in the Pentateuch about how Moses was allowed only to glimpse *the hind parts of God* after much pleading on his part (Ex. 33:17ff). Does the recipient of the theophany see with the physical eyes or with the eyes of the mind or with some other kind of transcendent vision?

In the Old Testament the same verb we meet in the resurrection narratives is used where the prophet says,

"God appeared unto me and said. . . ." No one would suggest that these Old Testament phrases mean that God was visible to the physical eye. Indeed, the Old Testament in its passion against idolatry suggests that no one can see God and live. Yet the prophetic recipient of these experiences with Yahweh did not doubt for a moment the reality of these revelatory encounters. They were revelations not from heaven above, as our limited vocabulary and time–space-shaped language seemed to imply, but revelations from the timeless sphere of eternity, from the eschatological realm into the present. This is clearly the sense of the verb translated "appeared" in 1 Corinthians 15:5–7, Luke 24:34, and throughout the book of Acts. If we would grasp the full significance of this insight, we must seek to understand and comprehend the way the Jewish mind of the first century thought about these subjects.

When a first-century Jew thought about life after death, he inevitably had both his understanding and his vocabulary shaped by that which we call Jewish apocalyptic literature. This is a term used to describe a style of thinking and writing popular at that time. We meet this style of writing overtly in parts of the book of Daniel, which is a second-century B.C. work. It is also used in the intertestamental book of Enoch and finds its most obvious expression in the New Testament in the book of Revelation and in Mark 13, Matthew 24, and Luke 17, yet it has shaped and influenced the entire New Testament perspective. Apocalyptic literature pictorially described the end of the world, that moment beyond history when all of life would be brought to its final conclusion which preceded the dawn of a new age beyond time. This general resurrection was seen as the presupposition for carrying out the last judgment. The emphasis was not so much on the fate of the dead as on the justice of God. As the faithful Jew would pray, "Blessed art thou, Oh Lord, that quickenest the dead." This apocalyptic writing style was full of symbols, dreams, cryptic words and phrases.

Yet in this literature there is a very specific concept of life after death. God is the creator, and he will keep faith with his creation. He does not withdraw his yes to life. At the decisive moment of death, he adds another yes to his first one. When the end of this world would come, which the apocalypticist expected imminently, a new age, which was beyond history, would be born. At that moment (to use a time-oriented word to describe that which is beyond time), the living and the dead would undergo a transformation. There would be a new birth through which the living and the dead would enter that new realm of reality that is beyond the limits of both time and space. The dead would not be restored to life or resurrected into life; they would rather be translated, and the living would be changed.

Paul was under the influence of this apocalyptic idea when he wrote, "We shall all be changed in a moment, in the twinkling of an eye." The transformation into this new being was thought to be so total that Paul could draw a pointed contrast, "We are sown in dishonor but raised in glory; we are sown in weakness but raised in power; we are sown a physical body but raised a spiritual body." The dead will be raised imperishable, of a new order, participating in a new creation, a new being. This apocalyptic hope was not attached to a moment of history nor to an event in time. It was specifically beyond history and at the end of time.

Almost certainly a first-century Jew, when he thought of resurrection, and most particularly of individual resurrection, would think in these terms. Martha in the Fourth Gospel's story of Lazarus said to Jesus, "Lord, I know he (Lazarus) will live again at the general resurrection on the last day." All of the disciples were Jewish men whose minds had been shaped by the apocalyptic hope; hence, whatever they experienced on Easter and whenever they dated the Easter Moment would inevitably be understood in these concepts. So Easter dawned, and they began to say that the moment that was supposed to take place at the end of history somehow in Jesus of Nazareth had been experienced in history. Or at the very least that the Easter Moment was a promise, a foretaste of that eschatological, posthistoric moment of transformation into a new creation for both the living and the dead. This is to suggest that the Easter Moment, which they called Resurrection, was, in fact, a revelatory encounter of the living God seen raising Jesus as a guarantee of the reality of the age to come when the dead shall be raised and the living shall be changed and the Kingdom of Heaven will dawn. If this context is the proper interpretive framework in which Easter is to be understood, then physical appearances inside history (please note the word physical) have to be a later exaggeration by and for landlocked minds and eyes that could not embrace the startling wonder of the Easter Moment.[14]

Hints of this apocalyptic, metahistorical understanding of the Easter Moment punctuate the New Testament. The angels who announced the Resurrection at the tomb would immediately be read by first-century Jewish people to be apocalyptic interpreting angels, for their appearance and activity are described in the exact terms of the contemporary apocalyptic literature. In the book of Revelation Jesus is called "the firstborn of the dead," a clear apocalyptic reference. Paul calls Jesus "the first fruits of them that slept." His death was seen to be analogous to the end of the world. "There was darkness over the whole land," and whatever took place on Easter came to be thought of as analogous to or the first instance of what the ultimate resurrection at the last day would be. The events of crucifixion and Easter were seen to be of cosmic and universal significance. "As in Adam all die, even so in Christ shall all be made alive," wrote Paul. When we add to this the suggestion made previously that the final resurrection would take place on the third day after the end of history, we find a chronological harmony with the resurrection narratives.

Let us be sure we understand what this does and does not point to. It certainly does not suggest that the Easter narratives were contrived and do not possess reality. Easter cannot be nothing, or fictitious, or imaginary. In the most profound sense it must be a real event. But what Easter is bursts through and goes beyond the bounds of history. It is a transcendental happening in which God raised Jesus out of death into his own all-embracing dimension. It does point inevitably to the overwhelming conclusion that the apocalyptic expectation so popular among Jewish thinkers in the first century has, in fact, shaped not the experience of Easter which no language can shape, but the rational understanding of the experience of Easter. That is a crucial distinction. It does suggest that these apocalyptic concepts organized the details of the Easter story.

Something happened at the Easter Moment. Whatever it was that happened had to be described in the limited words and language of those who shared that experience. Inevitably, the historic details and the historic words used to describe and explain this Moment can never capture this Moment. For this Moment is beyond history, beyond finitude, beyond time, but somehow in some way it was experienced in history by finite people who are captured by time and limited by finitude. We might measure the impact on the recipient, but we can never measure that which created the impact.

I am further encouraged in this conclusion by the fact that Paul never in all his writing narrates or shares with his readers the content of his own conversion, which he calls a resurrection experience. He *assumes* it. His life reflects it. His activities make no sense apart from it. But he never talks about it. It remained for Luke, writing in the book of Acts some twenty-five to thirty years after Paul's death, to create a narration of the details we know as the Damascus Road story. Paul probably would not recognize it. It is quite interesting to note that Paul never mentions Ananias whom Luke suggests played so determinative a role in Paul's conversion.

All of this suggests to me that the Easter Moment was neither an appearance nor a vision but a revelatory encounter. It was a moment when a truth beyond the truths of men and women was perceived. It was a mind-expanding, eye-opening experience which forced those who shared it to identify Jesus of Nazareth with that apocalyptic power called the Son of Man who was to herald the end of this age. The idea of the resurrection of the Messiah was a startlingly new idea even inside the apocalyptic tradition. The idea of the resurrection of a messiah who had failed, who was victim not victor, broke through all of the apocalyptic imagery, was an absolute novelty in the Jewish tradition, and remains unacceptable today for Judaism even among those Jews who believe in life after death.

Yet this was the only way the disciples could explain what they had experienced. The Moment of Easter began with the sudden realization that Jesus' death had cosmic significance. Something happened in his death that convinced this group of witnesses that what they expected to come at the end of the world had, in fact, been perceived now in Jesus with minds that still were limited by time and space and history. In Jesus they suddenly saw a new order of creation, and no longer was this realm in doubt. No longer was it even an object of speculation. Something about Jesus had tested all of the barriers of human existence in his life. He was free to live, to love, and to be. He could give himself away recklessly, totally. He had no need to defend or enhance his being. He could meet life on levels far beneath the superficial. He could penetrate beyond those inevitable human defense barriers and explore life in its depths. He could reach the very DNA of life. Now in his death he had tested the ultimate barrier, the ultimate limit of human life. Those who knew him and those who shared the Easter Moment were convinced beyond any shadows of doubt that he had opened to them and to all who are or will be *in Christ* both a view and a means of passage into that realm forever.

When the Fourth Gospel has the Christ say, "I am the way, the truth, and the life. No one comes to the father but by me" (Jn. 14:6), he is not making an exclusive Jesus claim to bolster later ecclesiastical, imperialistic missionary tactics. He is referring to the cosmic significance for all life of the Christ figure who in the

Easter Moment revealed the truth of the timeless eternity of God and our way of sharing in that timeless eternity. God had raised him, revealing him to be both Lord and Christ, for his was the divine life that had opened to all humanity the new world, the new vision, and the transformed realm of new being. Those who came to share in his power found that they could participate in that realm now before death, before the end of the world. The person who is *in Christ* could live, as the New Testament suggests, in this world but by the power of the world to come. Easter was a ringing confirmation that beyond the limit of our eyes or the touch of our hands there was an eternal, timeless reality. Jesus is the door (Jn. 10:9), says the Fourth Gospel. He is the Resurrection (Jn. 11:25), the life (Jn. 11:25), the living water (Jn. 4:7ff), the bread of life (Jn. 6:35). All of the *I AM* claims of the Fourth Gospel are meant primarily to illumine the one central Easter claim: he lives and because he lives, you and I can live in a new way, a way we never dreamed possible. All of this is involved in the Easter Moment.

We have opened the doors to a reality that is beyond objectivity and history but which nonetheless was known by first-century people who were both subjective and historic. It remains now to press one step closer to that Easter Moment. What caused them to see this? What startled them and opened their eyes to see what they had never seen before? What enabled them to view life and Jesus in a dramatic new way? What forced them to see Jesus as included in God and God as including Jesus? For that is what Easter did.

Chapter 17

A Possible Reconstruction
(Part 1)

It is not resurrection per se that gives focus and direction to the Christian Church or the New Testament. It is rather the Resurrection of Jesus of Nazareth that is center stage. To understand, indeed to enter, this crucial Easter Moment, we must somehow enter the mind of this Jesus, or at the very least the mind of the early church about this Jesus.

Questions abound. Was it the mighty acts of his power that caused people to see God in Jesus of Nazareth, or was it because they saw God in Jesus of Nazareth that they attributed to him mighty acts of power? What was the content of the Moment when they knew that they could never again think of God without seeing him as included in all that the word God meant? To identify that Moment is to define Easter, To enter that Moment is to enter Easter.

In this chapter we will seek to isolate it, explore it, enter it; for the heart of the Gospel lies here. If Jesus did not rise, there is no resurrection, says Paul; and if there is no resurrection, then your faith is in vain, and we (Christians) of all people are most to be pitied.

Recall that no verse of the New Testament is written save as a post-Easter phenomenon. So every narrative about Jesus, every word, saying, and parable of Jesus, every healing episode involving Jesus is an account of an episode in the life of one acknowledged by the church and worshiped as the resurrected, ascended, glorified Lord. When we realize that every verse is a post-Easter verse, then new meanings flow from these ancient and familiar texts.

The Gospels portray Jesus as one who had an unbroken sense of oneness with God and an intensive awareness of this reality at every moment of his existence. Paul proclaimed this simply: "God was in Christ."

The explanation of the meaning of this Jesus took the entire first century to work out canonically and almost six centuries to work out creedally. But explanations are always after the fact. How God was in Christ could be endlessly debated. That in Jesus they had met God in a unique, decisive way was clearly the first Christians' undoubted experience. They saw Jesus as one who possessed the infinite freedom of wholeness. He was portrayed as possessing the intuitive power of an uncanny insight. He could read the lives of others as if they were an open book. He could communicate even with those who were thought to be mentally deranged or demon-possessed. He lived in a vivid receptivity and in a total communion with the holy. This sense of the holy he found not only in God but also at the very heart and in the very depth of human life.

True to his Hebrew heritage, God and life were not separated categories. God was always a verb. God and love, God and being could not be surgically parted. Yahweh, the name given God in the burning bush story of the book of Exodus, is best translated, my Jewish friends tell me, by something like "I am that which causes all that is to be." It was this sense of the holy God met in the center of life that enabled Jesus to see even the commonplace things of existence with an artist's intensity of apprehension. He was totally available to every human being he confronted. Never is Jesus portrayed as looking over his shoulder at the next moment in time. He exhausted the wonder of every moment. The whole of his being, the full capacity of his power was lived out constantly. His ability to give life and to give love seemed infinite. Even when his life was being taken away, he is not pictured as grasping or clinging but giving willingly and freely.

All of this is portrayed in the New Testament as a pre-Easter description of Jesus. It is rather a post-Easter memory. I do not mean to suggest that it is an inaccurate memory, but there is no way the Easter Moment could not have shaped and informed this memory. Jesus' identity as the risen Lord was far too dramatic a part of his being not to have colored even the most vivid recollections.

But the Gospels are equally clear in their assertion that during the course of Jesus' earthly life no other human being perceived, recognized, or shared in the true meaning and nature of this Christ until the Moment of Easter. So on the lowest level of meaning and at the very least, Easter was the Moment when the disciples were able to see, to understand, to participate in his life, to share in his power. Easter was the Moment when the confines of their minds were broken open and they saw that in Jesus of Nazareth the full reality of God and the deepest truth about human life were not only revealed but were beckoning and inviting them to enter, to participate, and to live in the power of that meaning. I am convinced that Easter was infinitely more than this, but we must begin by looking at this moment subjectively.

What brought the disciples to see the truth of Jesus beyond the fact of the crucifixion? What enabled them to be certain that beyond the death of Jesus they had seen the living Christ? What forced open their eyes? What required, indeed demanded, of them that they identify the Jesus of history whom they had known in the flesh and loved as an earthly companion and teacher with the apocalyptic figure called the Son of Man who would usher in the dawn of a new creation? What brought these disciples to proclaim, "He is not here; he is risen!" and to proclaim it with such power and such conviction that their lives were never the same and that the history of their world was never the same? What removed their earthbound, time-limited blinders so that in an ecstatic moment of incredulous wonder they could see in Jesus both God and the fullness of human life and see all things anew in the splendor of transcendence and eternity? That is what the Easter Moment did!

I think the clue to this is so simple that its very simplicity baffled and embarrassed the members of the early church. Its lack of profundity all but cried out for an embellishment of the account and a heightening of the miraculous in the narrative. Yet at the same time this truth was so real and so etched upon their unforgettable memory that it echoed over and over throughout the New Testament record.

Think for a moment about the place of the sacramental meal in Christian history. Why did this become the major worship symbol for Christian people from the very beginning? Search the biblical narrative, and see what a powerful place the sacramental common meal has in the Gospel narrative. Matthew, Mark, and Luke all include accounts of the last supper, and to it they assign a place of incredible significance. The Fourth Gospel omits the last supper narrative and substitutes the story of Jesus' washing the disciples' feet. But this is done, I am convinced, because in John's mind Jesus on the cross became the *bread of life broken for you*. This is proved to my satisfaction by the Fourth Gospel's having the Christ say, "I am the bread of life; he who comes to me shall not hunger" (Jn. 6:35). The Fourth Gospel also attaches all of its highly developed sacramental teaching to the story of Jesus' feeding of the 5,000. I think that it is not coincidental that the only miraculous event other than Easter that all four Gospels record is the account of a miraculous feeding of the multitude. Why did that story gather more attention about it than any other?

When these several versions of the miraculous feeding of the multitude are isolated and read, they are obviously full of symbols. The careful numbering of the crowd: 5,000 men (the Bible could not escape its cultural chauvinism), on another occasion 4,000. Five loaves once, seven loaves later. Twelve baskets of fragments were gathered in one account on the Jewish side of the lake. Later on the Gentile side seven baskets of fragments remained. The eucharistic verbs so obviously shaped by the liturgy are employed by the authors: Jesus took the bread, blessed it or gave thanks for it, broke it, and gave it. Paul, giving us the earliest version of the last supper, employs the same four verbs in the exact order.

What is it that the evangelists are saying in the re-telling of what appears to be a simple miracle story? Was this a literal historic episode, a miraculous feeding of a multitude by a first-century wonderworker? I doubt it, and I know of no contemporary New Testament scholar who would treat any version of the miraculous feeding stories as if they were descriptions of objective history. Was this a parable about the inexhaustible power of the risen Christ who was beyond all of the limitations of time and space read back as a narrative event in the life of the pre-Easter Jesus? I would bet my life on it, and here and in many other places, which I shall seek to document, I find the clue that for me unlocks the content of the Moment in which the disciples' eyes were opened to see the risen Lord.

Time and time again the resurrection narratives of the New Testament combine the appearance of the risen Christ and the experience of eating together. I cannot agree with those who dismiss these accounts simply as an attempt to demonstrate or to heighten the physical reality of resurrection. In the later, and as we have seen contradictory, resurrection narrations that the Gospels include, that may well be a motive, even a primary motive, for portraying the risen Christ as eating; but the connection is too deep, too significant to be so categorically and cavalierly treated. Why did the earliest Christian tradition decide to use the eating of food as the means to heighten the physical reality of the resurrected one? Can people create a tradition out of nothing—a tradition so powerful that even today, 2,000 years later, Christians meet to worship inside the experience of a common meal. This meal finds expression in highly stylized liturgical forms ranging from a fellowship-oriented Lord's Supper in a country Baptist Church in the American South to a pontifical high mass at St. Peter's basilica in Rome. Wherever the physical location is and no matter how simple or how complex the ritual, whenever the church has gathered to worship the Risen Christ, it has done so with the sharing of a meal that has a sacramental meaning. How did the idea of sacrament and meal become so closely linked?

We examine first the food references in the resurrection narratives of the New Testament. In the Emmaus Road story (Lk. 24:13ff) the risen Christ is at first not perceived. He is thought to be a stranger. As they walked the road to Emmaus, the account suggests that this stranger tried to show that suffering and dying did not preclude being the messiah, but Cleopas and his friend did not understand. Finally, they sat down to eat the evening meal. The stranger took bread, blessed it, broke it, gave it. Immediately, says Luke, "Their eyes were opened," and they recognized him. He vanished out of their sight. These disciples returned to Jerusalem to inform the others. They did so, says Luke, with the words "he was made known to them in the breaking of bread" (Lk. 24:35). Almost immediately Luke has the risen Christ appear again even as they discussed these wondrous events. He asked, "Have you anything to eat?" (Lk. 24:41).

In the opening verses of the book of Acts (Acts 1:4), is recorded, "And as he (the risen Lord) was *eating* with them, he charged them not to depart from Jerusalem but to wait for the promise of the Father." Later in Acts (10:41) in one of the sermons of Peter, Peter is made to say that the risen Christ appeared "to those of us who *ate* and *drank* with Him."

In the book of Revelation (3:20) the risen Christ is portrayed as standing at the doorway of our lives and knocking. The author in a very interesting verb usage says that if we open the door, he will come in and *dine* or *sup* or *eat* with us. To the mind of the early church, that was the appropriate verb to describe the presence of the Christ being experienced.

In the Fourth Gospel in a note referred to earlier in this volume, chapter 8, the resurrection appearance is set at the time of the evening meal. One week later when Thomas was present, the risen Christ appeared once more at the time of the evening meal. In the twenty-first chapter of John, Jesus is revealed to his disciples as they ate together on the shore of the Sea of Galilee. Then he confronted Peter in a dialogue that turned on two verbs, love and feed. If you love, Peter, you will feed.

In these fragments of the resurrection narrative, I believe there is preserved the original context in which the meaning and the power of Easter were first experienced. If I had to reconstruct the Easter Moment as it dawned on the disciples, I would suggest that it looked something like this. For some time, perhaps as long as three years, the disciples had gathered around the man from Nazareth named Jesus. What he meant to each of them at that moment we can never be certain, but it is fair to assume that they were not trinitarians or dogmatic theologians and that they were not disposed to think of Jesus in any category save human. Yet over and over again the human capacities by which they sought to measure him had to be expanded. Why each of them wandered into the disciple relationship is forever lost, but we may safely assume a variety of reasons. Doubtless some of them, perhaps including Judas, saw in Jesus earthly messianic possibilities. Some of them were looking for success and saw Jesus as the star to which they should hitch their wagons. If the title zealot is historically accurate in its application to Simon, then surely he saw in Jesus a revolutionary movement to which he wanted to be attached. It is quite clear that the Jesus movement was basically a Galilean movement. The very clear Gospel tradition shows the Jesus movement to have its origins in Galilee.[15]

Jesus first achieved public notice, it appears, on two counts: his teaching and his acts of healing. His public ministry was undoubtedly inaugurated when he was baptized by John in the River Jordan. The difficulty the early Christians had interpreting that event was obvious. Surely they would not have invented a narrative that created that much of an apologetic problem. The baptism seems to have been a crucial moment for him. Each of the Gospels gives us a version of the impact of that moment on Jesus. But remember, we have the benefit of tradition; they did not. For them each day added to the tradition the meaning, the understanding they were to pass on to us.

What the disciples saw and experienced was that this Jesus possessed an uncanny power. I am quite certain that it was not, at least at first, what even they would call miraculous power. It was rather the power of a self-assured authority, the power of insight, the power of a secure, whole person, the power of one who possessed radical and existential freedom. They could not help being aware that his life stood in strange contrast to their own. They were anxious; he was at peace.

They were grasping to become; he was content to be. They were jealous of their status; he was able to embrace children, lepers, and all sorts of others who were not capable of enhancing him. Somehow he had no need to be enhanced. They cited their credentials; Jesus said simply, "Verily I say unto you." Constantly his scandalized critics shouted, "By what authority do you say or do these things?" The disciples were always concerned about the next day; Jesus was able to be totally present in the *now*. I suspect that this was the first reality they perceived, and interestingly enough these qualities—freedom, security, wholeness—are still both magnetically attractive and threateningly fearful.

Jesus had one other capacity that seemed to set him apart in the minds of the disciples, and that was his standard of judgment, a standard by which they benefited; for only one who operated on this standard would ever have chosen these particular men for discipleship. Jesus seems to have seen all persons not as they were, and certainly not as they ought to be, but rather as they could be, given the one ingredient that broken human life seems so desperately to require— healing, accepting, forgiving, affirming love. It is the kind of love that finally only God can give, and yet time and again the disciples seem to have experienced exactly this kind of love from Jesus of Nazareth.

Jesus was also uniquely and intensely related to God, and this too must have been obvious. Jesus knew God in a disquietingly familiar way. We cannot get inside his prayer life, but we can see enormous power there. It was Irenaeus who observed in A.D. 175 that "the glory of God is man fully alive."[16] But Jesus seems to have lived out what Irenaeus articulated. It was unmistakable yet never analyzed or articulated by the disciples. They experienced it, they grew in it, they were mystified by it. His fully alive life had depth and power, and the more deeply they perceived it, the more of God's glory they perceived in it.

How Jesus understood himself no one can ever say with authority. But it is fair to say that something happened in Jesus' baptism that set in motion the course of his entire life. The wilderness experience we call the temptation was his own attempt to understand what the baptism seemed to have made clear to him, namely, that in some strange and mysterious way God was acting in human history through him. He recognized that he had a unique vocation: on God's behalf to restore God's creation to the wholeness that God intended. Jesus perceived God as restorative power. God was worshiped when the fullness of life emerged from the brokenness of humanity. The wholeness that Jesus knew himself to possess was what God intended for all his children. He was called, ordained, created, empowered to offer to the world the wholeness of God, the fullness of life, the power of love.[17]

How that power came to Jesus, when it became part of Jesus' identity, only God knows. I would say, though, that no one finally can become something or someone that he never was, so that John's prologue hymn of praise to the preexistent logos is for me the most satisfying Christological statement. However, as we attempt to retrace this drama, our purpose is not to prove Christology but to see how it dawned upon the consciousness of the people involved in the drama.

Jesus understood the messianic purpose to be to bring God—life, love, being, wholeness—to distorted, broken, insecure, grasping human life. He accepted that vocation self-consciously at his baptism. The

Fourth Gospel accurately captures this when it has him say, "I have come that you might have life abundantly." He tested this vocation in the wilderness and dismissed as temptation the popular understandings of where wholeness can be found. It is not found in the meeting of physical needs: "Man does not live by bread alone." It is not found in meeting status needs: "Worship me and all the kingdoms of the world will be yours." It is not found in meeting religious needs, acting as if you can manipulate God to show favoritism. "The family that prays together, stays together" is the modern version of the ancient temptation, "Cast yourself off the pinnacle of the temple, Jesus, for he will give his angels charge concerning you lest you dash your foot against a stone." Wholeness, the fullness of life, results only when the infinite love of God embraces and restores the brokenness of human life.

Jesus seemed to understand and to see the infinite love of God to be his unique gift to bring, and his commitment to bring it was his call to be messiah. His vocation set him apart. In classical theological terms his ability to bring God totally was his claim to a divine nature, and his ability to live out the presence of God through his unbroken humanity was his claim to a perfect human nature. Like all theological terms, *Jesus the God–man* is a finite, frail, human attempt to make sense out of the reality of the experience that all that God meant was met, engaged, and worshiped in this Jesus who never ceased to be fully and completely human. When we get behind the words, we do not argue; we are rather drawn into mystery, awe, wonder, worship. That did not dawn suddenly on anyone. Yet every time they thought they understood, something happened that broke the barriers of their minds, and they saw how inadequate their understandings had been. In the life of the disciples it was an ongoing process.

Perhaps it was in Jesus' mind also. It is one thing to be aware of your purpose and quite another to know clearly how you will accomplish that purpose. The temptation story reveals a wrestling with alternatives that were rejected as inadequate. It is safe to assume that this inner wrestling continued not with the employment of the inadequate and rejected alternatives but with alternatives that were adequate but unsuccessful. The unsuccessful note lay in the inability of the disciples to discern their meaning, not in the inadequacy of the method.

Jesus was a teacher. His teaching was designed to illumine in his hearers the meaning of the purpose of his life. His teachings pointed to the results that are achieved when life is embraced in the recreating power of the love of God. That is what it means to be in the kingdom of God. When perfect love embraces life, those security-producing but mindless prejudices will disappear; so listen to the parable of the good Samaritan. When the infinite worth of human life is experienced, then the limited standards of human judgment are transcended. Prodigal sons are embraced, lost sheep are searched out and found, talents are multiplied. When the love of God touches human life, the capacity to give is enhanced, and it is the capacity to give, not the amount that is given, that becomes a mark of the kingdom. So watch for the widow and her mite.

On and on went the teaching ministry of this Jesus. Surely they would hear, see, and respond. But that is never the result. Men and women hear only out of the blindness of their needs. Some thought he was a rabble-rouser, fit only to be banished. Others thought

181

he should be made king so that his wisdom could rule the nation. If Jesus ever entertained the hope that his teaching could enable men and women to see the meaning of his life and to be embraced by the power of his love, then surely the response he encountered must have dismayed and disappointed him. Teaching was not to be the means through which his messianic vocation could be accomplished.

There was another alternative. The power of the infinite love of God recreates wholeness when it touches the brokenness of human life. If Jesus possessed this power, then he would act it out. Twisted bodies would be made whole, distorted and deranged minds would be restored. There is no doubt in my mind that the New Testament portrait of Jesus as capable of doing wondrous acts of healing is accurate. Details may be heightened. The original diagnosis may not have been accurate. People who are convinced that epilepsy, schizophrenia, and deaf muteness are the result of demon-possession might well have no better understanding of how such afflictions are cured. But Jesus touched lives that were broken or distorted, and a wondrous wholeness resulted. "Devils are banished"; that is a sign that the kingdom of God is upon you.

Jesus did not *do miracles* to prove his divinity. But miracles, that is, marvelous acts that defied traditional limitations of explanation, did mark his life. Perhaps he hoped that people's eyes would be opened by these signs and that they would see, experience, and believe the power with which he was endowed—the power to act out God's healing love in human history.

But did they see? Of course not. Once again blinded by their own needs, some saw in him a wonderworker who perhaps could be manipulated to suit their purposes. Others saw a demon-possessed man who did these mighty acts by the power of Beelzebub, and they wanted to banish him. Jesus tried to speak to that ("A kingdom divided against itself will not stand"), but it was to no avail. The meaning of the life-giving, recreating love of God was being demonstrated in their very midst. But the people who had ears to hear his teaching did not hear, and those who had eyes to see his inner meaning acted out did not see. Mighty acts of healing were not to be the means through which his messianic vocation would be accomplished.

There was another alternative. Perhaps it was too much to expect the masses of people who constituted the ever-present crowd to comprehend. They did not really know this Jesus. His words, his actions were somewhat isolated in their minds from his person. They responded to his public image, which is always a distortion. So Jesus narrowed his scope and concentrated not on the crowds but on the intimate circle of his disciples. He would show them, teach them, and live with them in a community that was so deep, so intimate that they would hear his words and view his actions in the context of sharing completely in his life. Perhaps they would then understand.

In the Fourth Gospel between the Lazarus story and the events of Holy Week a long section is included that is called *the farewell discourses*. In Luke there is a section between the time Jesus set his face to Jerusalem and the time he arrived that consumed a significant part of Luke's text, called *the travel section*. In both of these biblical narratives the primary action is between Jesus and his disciples. They differ vastly in content as well as style. Both, however, seem to me to be the place where the memory of Jesus' intense relationship with the disciples is recalled. At some point he appears to turn away from the crowds and toward his chosen ones. He shared his thoughts, he interpreted his actions, he tried to open their eyes to understand his power. I think we cannot overestimate the intensity of that shared time, and yet the result Jesus seemed to hope for did not occur. The disciples, blinded by their own inner needs, simply did not see, perhaps could not see. Instead of sharing in Jesus' freedom, they debated as to which one of them would be greatest. They schemed even against each other.

Over and over again Jesus reached out to show them something more. Freedom, wholeness, and being do not have to be jealous, defensive, or status-conscious. The full and whole person can wash the feet of his inferiors, take the lowest seats at the banquet, or love one another as he has been loved. But the disciples never understood this, and when the last act of Jesus' great drama unfolded, the disciples could not overcome their own security needs. Acting out of what they obviously conceived of as their best interests, one of them betrayed Jesus, one of them denied him, and all the others forsook him and fled. The intimate association of Jesus with his disciples did not prove to be the means through which his messianic vocation could be accomplished.

When Jesus gave up on the disciples' response as the means through which he could impart his life-giving love to the world, no one can say. Some might suggest that when he took Peter, James, and John, his most trusted inner three, to the Garden of Gethsemane on the night of his arrest this was his last attempt to avoid the final alternative. If the disciples even at this moment could have understood, realized the source of the power of his life, allowed that power to be born in them, perhaps even then the cross might not have been necessary. Certainly the prayers of Jesus in the garden appear to be the moment when he knew there was no alternative. To accomplish his purpose of being the life through which God acts with his redeeming and re-creating love in human history was to do the will of the Father. That purpose his words, his actions, his association with the twelve had not achieved. Only one other alternative lay before him.

I am convinced that Jesus entertained this possibility from the very beginning. Long before he launched his public career, he obviously steeped himself in his scriptures. Embedded in those scriptures were the servant songs of the book of Isaiah. Written in the sixth century B.C. to sketch a new vocation or to interpret the present vocation of the post-exilic people of God who possessed no power, no grandeur, no splendor, these songs portrayed a servant who was weak, defeated, abused, killed; and yet by being faithful, even as a victim he was vindicated and became a light to lighten the nations and the glory of Israel. Perhaps Jesus saw the role of the servant as another means of accomplishing his purpose. Perhaps what men and women could not hear in his words or see in his actions or experience in the intimacy of their life together they would be able to see and hear and experience if he lived out self-consciously the role of the servant. But for there to be any chance of accomplishing his purpose, the disciples would have to understand, to interpret correctly, and in the power of that action to experience the meaning, the love, the freedom of his life.

When any of these thoughts became Jesus' purpose no one can say. I suspect that this was always an option, but never until the very end of his life was it his only option. I am also convinced it became his only option, not by his choice but rather by the fact that the disciples successively closed the doors on every other possibility.

The servant must act out the meaning of his life at the center of the stage. It must not occur in some remote region, so Jesus was careful not to be arrested in Galilee or to have his final showdown at some insignificant moment. Rather he set his face "like flint," says St. Luke, for Jerusalem at the time of the crowded, nationalistically oriented festival of the Passover. Whatever else the Gospels say, it is quite clear that Jesus directed every detail of these final days of his life. The preparation for the challenge of Palm Sunday and the last supper was elaborate. Obviously some advance work had been accomplished. A sign had been given. A donkey for the procession was available. A large upper room, furnished, had been made ready. A retreat to safety in Bethany had been prepared. How else could one interpret this elaborate detail preserved in the earliest Christian records called the passion narrative? Then according to plan the drama unfolded.

The Palm Sunday procession from the Mount of Olives to Jerusalem achieved public attention. It was nothing less than a street demonstration. The cleansing of the temple of the moneychangers was the gauntlet thrown down at the feet of the religious hierarchy. The retreat to Bethany for the night guaranteed the proper time schedule. The public teaching to responsive crowds in the daylight hours heightened the tension and the anger. The attempt to pry loose one of his intimate circle was an appropriate response.

Finally, the night of the final meal came. Matthew,

Mark, and Luke say it was the Passover. John says not so. It really does not matter. All Jewish meals have religious contexts, and this one, whether Passover or not, was caught up in the drama of that week. That is an inescapable fact. The disciples were on an emotional merry-go-round. All of their own nationalistic feelings and messianic hopes must have been fired by the events of Palm Sunday. There was no mistaking the messianic symbol of Jesus' entry into Jerusalem riding on an ass. Zechariah's words were popular and well-known. The shouts of "Hosannah to the Son of David" and "Blessed is he who comes in the name of the Lord" both had significant messianic meanings. But before the flow of these moments could subside, there was Jesus in the temple, casting out the moneychangers. No one was blind to the authorities' rage, and the disciples were fearful, wondering, confused. As the week wore on, the atmosphere became more and more taut. Judas' defection was already a private but not yet a public fact. Finally, it all culminated in that upper room on that day we call Maundy Thursday.

The mood was melancholy. The room was, in a sense, a hideout. Fear was pervasive. Death seemed omnipresent. In this setting they prepared to eat. This may have been the first night since Palm Sunday that Jesus and his disciples had risked remaining in Jerusalem. The record is silent on the nightly abode, but the careful attention Jesus gave to the events of this week would cause one to suspect that a plan for nightly sanctuary outside Jerusalem was not overlooked. The disciples gathered on the reclining benches. The meal began.

Jesus, serving as host or head of the family, initiated the meal with the blessing of bread. It was in the tradition of Jewish meals that the head of the household could add the special meaning to each dinner beyond the significance the meal traditionally had. Hence, Jesus' ad-libbing on the text was normal but nonetheless added its own ominous note. He took bread, raised his eyes heavenward, blessed God giving thanks for the bread, and then he broke it. As he broke it, he added words identifying that broken bread with his body, which would be broken for them. It was a strange note, a new note. They must have wondered what he meant. Remember that with pre–Good Friday understandings it was not at all obvious what it was he meant. The earliest version we have of this supper is in Paul (1 Cor. 11:23ff.) where Paul uses the formula reserved for the most ancient and authentic versions of the Christian tradition. Paul writes, "For I have received of the Lord that which also I delivered unto you, That the Lord Jesus, the same night in which he was betrayed, took bread: and when he had given thanks, he broke it, and said, 'Take, eat; this is my body, which is broken for you.'" And here Paul adds words, which I am convinced are both authentic and crucial, *"This do in remembrance of me."* Luke alone of the Gospels includes this command in his narration of that unusual meal.

If the traditional pattern was followed, as Paul suggests it was, the meal followed that blessing. I suspect it was eaten in a somber mood. The gaity of Passover was certainly not the spirit of this evening. The meal having ended, Jesus again presiding took the cup of wine. Once more he blessed God, giving thanks for the fruit of the vine. Then offering the cup he identified its contents with his blood shed for them to inaugurate a new covenant with God. Once more, Paul says, he enjoined them, "As oft as you drink it, do this in remembrance of me. For as often as you eat this bread and drink this cup, you do show forth the Lord's death until he comes."

Broken bread. This is my body. Poured-out wine. This is my blood. The synoptics suggest that after they sang a hymn the meal ended and the drama rolled on toward its crescendo. The Garden of Gethsemane, the betrayal, the arrest, the trial, the torture, the march to Calvary, the crucifixion all followed in rapid succession.

What was Jesus doing at that last supper? Was he trying to make them understand even then what his ministry among them for whatever its duration had failed to make them understand? Or did he by then know that for him to accomplish his messianic purpose he must suffer death? He wanted to give them this mighty interpretive clue through which they might understand his death and through that understanding come to experience the meaning of his life. He was going to live out the meaning of the love of God in the face of every human distortion of that love. The brokenness of human life would inevitably make this kind of love its victim. That was the fate of the servant about whom Isaiah wrote; the meaning of his life would never be born in them.

So at the last supper even though they did not understand, he gave them a clue, an interpretive clue that would unlock both the meaning and the power of his life. And to prevent them from misunderstanding or missing this clue altogether, his final word was do this whenever you gather to eat again; do this in remembrance of me. See my life under the symbols of broken bread, poured-out wine.

We watch Jesus walk through those final moments of

his life. We observe his freedom, his life, his love, his unlimited capacity to give. We watch him absorb abuse and return love, absorb hate and return forgiveness, absorb misunderstanding and return acceptance. He was betrayed, and he loved the betrayer. He was denied, and he loved the denier. He was abused, and he responded by loving the abusers. Never did he grasp at the straws of life. Complete, whole, he laid his life down, a willing, loving victim. He was dying, and yet he ministered to the needs of those who were still alive. To the soldiers he spoke the word of forgiveness, to the thief the word of assurance, to his mother the word of caring. Here a dying form suspended from a cross lived out the freedom, the wholeness, the fullness of life that only one in touch with the meaning of God could possibly possess. He died. People watched. The disciples seemed to have scattered, but to where we do not know. Peter did linger to watch, to deny, to weep. The drama was over.

Most people felt the final curtain had rung down on this life. Perhaps they discussed him, perhaps they by and large ignored him. But those who watched him die could not help wondering. It was a haunting kind of wonder. But no matter what avenue of thought they followed, it all ended at the same point. Jesus was dead. Executed by the religious hierarchy, the official spokesmen for God, for the crime of blasphemy. All hopes ended with his death, for God did not spare him. They could not comprehend a messiah who would be killed. The sun sank, the bodies were hastily removed and hastily buried. The watchman blew the shofar. The Sabbath had begun. It would probably be the longest Sabbath, at least for some of the disciples and especially for Peter.

Chapter 18

A Possible Reconstruction (Part 2)

It was the Sabbath—a day of rest and worship, a day when the God-consciousness of the Jewish man and woman was particularly intense. We must never forget that the disciples were all Jewish. Did they have time before the setting sun announced the arrival of the Sabbath to flee to the relative safety of Galilee? I suspect some did. I am convinced all did not. Peter had lingered to witness the arrest, the trial. My educated guess is that he was still in Jerusalem with a few of the others. Militating against departure was the fact that one could not journey more than three-fifths of a mile on the Sabbath without breaking the law. The story of Cleopas and his friend's journeying to Emmaus on the first day of the week seems to me to support the idea that at least some of the disciples waited until the Sabbath had passed to depart.

I suspect those that stayed gambled on three things. First, the authorities would feel that destroying the leader would destroy the movement; a purge of the followers was therefore not necessary. Second, the swollen city would soon be back to normal when the Passover pilgrims departed, and their best chance for escape lay in blending into the crowd and leaving when the crowd left. Finally, there was a security about the Sabbath. Jews did not arrest criminals on the Sabbath unless absolutely necessary, for that too was work.

So the disciples who remained observed the Sabbath, I believe. They worshiped, they prayed, they were as inconspicuous as possible. But if they were arrested, they would want to be able to demonstrate their strict adherence to the Sabbath tradition.

I suspect that the scattered group did not congregate on that day. They may well not have been in contact with one another. It was every man for himself or perhaps several groups of two or three. I think it is also essential to try to understand their feelings. There was grief. One they had known and loved was dead. There was fear. He had been executed by the civil and religious authorities, and perhaps they were next. There was confusion. Somehow they had never expected Jesus to conclude his public career in this fashion. There was perplexity. If he had been the messiah, he could not have died. He did die; therefore, he could not be the messiah.

There was a mind-set that had elements of the old Jewish idea of moral retribution against which Job had railed. There was a common assumption that God was in charge of the events of life and that one got what one deserved. In this episode it was expressed in the voices of the mob, "Let God save him!" If God had wanted to spare Jesus, he somehow could have. He did not. Therefore, he must not have wanted to do so. But how could God say no to Jesus, they wondered, for that would be like saying no to love, to forgiveness, and to life? Could the power of healing and wholeness that they had seen in Jesus have been unreal or demonic as his critics charged? Over and over they posed these questions as they tried to make sense out of the traumatic events of Friday. Jesus was dead. He had been crucified under Pontius Pilate. If they had hope of the Resurrection, it was a future hope at the end of history, the general resurrection at the last day. That did very little to ease their troubled minds or calm their fears or comfort them in the present moment of grief.

The Sabbath day wore on, and when the western sky began to record the day's end, a new problem emerged. Where would they spend the night? Where could they hide in relative security? Perhaps they had used the upper room on Friday night, but I doubt it. Judas obviously knew of it, and it did not seem a safe place in which to hide. If Judas' suicide is historic, it seems to have occurred by this time. Perhaps those who knew of it now felt the upper room to be safer. It would not surprise me if some of their belongings had been left there, belongings that they wanted to reclaim before returning to Galilee. For whatever reasons, some of the disciples, I am convinced, began to converge on that upper room for the night, for sanctuary on the first day of the week until they felt safe to depart.

I am also convinced that some of the disciples had fled on Thursday evening and were by this time already back in Galilee. This was by no means a cohesive group. This is hinted at by John who states that the disciples were not all present on the first Easter. Thomas specifically was not present. In the Johannine appendix

193

(chapter 21), only seven disciples are mentioned. In any event, some of the disciples gathered toward the evening hour or entered under cover of darkness into the relative sanctuary of that upper room.

When dawn broke, the women went to the tomb carrying the embalming spices to do the work that the Sabbath had prevented them from doing until this moment. What they found there I do not know, but it was enough to cause them to be disturbed. They reported this to the disciples. At that moment even an empty tomb would have conveyed more fear, not more faith. It would only mean that his enemies were not content to kill his body; now they had desecrated his grave. The few disciples who were in the upper room secured it as best they could. They locked the windows and barred the door. They waited more in silence than in comradeship at first. I doubt if they ate. Traumatized, grief-stricken people are not hungry. The hours passed. No knock was heard at their door, no voice that shouted, "Open up in the name of the law."

As time wore on, their internal security level began to rise, and they began to talk among themselves. I suspect that the content of their conversations was not unlike the conversations of most bereaved people who gather when their grief is fresh. They tried to understand. Why? they must have asked over and over. What meaning is there in these events? They shared their doubts, their fears, their questions, their grief. It is also common in bereavement to relive again and again the last time you were with the deceased. That would be easy in this setting, for that last time together was the meal eaten here. Now they saw it as the *Last* Supper. The table was still physically present. One does not wash dishes or clean up the kitchen on the Sabbath.

They discussed the strange conversation, the melancholy atmosphere. They retold Jesus' words, seeking to understand his meaning. Finally, as the afternoon wore on, their bodies began to send them hunger messages. They were welcomed, for they signaled a return to normalcy, a transition away from trauma.

Preparation was made for the evening meal, which was in Jerusalem an event of the late afternoon. Electricity had not yet created night life. When they gathered around that familiar table, maybe only three or four, Peter took charge. That was his nature. This was the first meal they had shared together since Thursday. Peter took the bread and began the ceremonial blessing. It was inevitable that Peter would refer to their last meal with Jesus, especially Jesus' command.

"You remember," began Peter, "that Jesus commanded us whenever we gathered together to break bread and to drink wine in memory of him. He told us that in this way we would show forth his death until he comes. So we gather now in our grief and observe what he commanded. On the night Jesus was betrayed," continued Peter, "he took bread. When he had given thanks, he broke the bread." At this point Peter broke it, tearing it dramatically into two pieces. With one in each hand Peter continued, and this broken bread he identified with his body, which would be broken for them. The wine he identified with his blood shed to inaugurate a new covenant.

Peter stopped and pondered the meaning of his own words. It was as if dawn was cracking the darkness of his mind. Suddenly, Peter looked at the cross through the symbols of broken bread and poured-out wine, and the cross looked radically different. Instantaneously, Peter recognized that Jesus was not the victim, that no one, not even God, had done this to him. The cross was not God's no to all that Jesus meant. It was rather a part of Jesus' plan. How else could he have let us know how deeply we are loved? We betrayed him, denied him, forsook him, and crucified him; and his response was to accept, to love, to forgive. The cross was the way he proclaimed to the world that there is nothing we can do and nothing we can be that will finally separate us from the love of God.

At that moment, for the first time, Peter, the one who denied, experienced the power and the depth of that love. He stepped into it. Peter was resurrected to new life, a new being. He saw life in a new way with all of its depth and wonder, its transcendence and ecstasy; and that opened his eyes. With those newly opened eyes Peter saw Jesus resurrected, alive. For that moment timelessness invaded time. The limitations of the human transitory state were overcome, and Jesus' death became the doorway into a realm of reality that constantly surrounds us but we never seem to see with our earthbound eyes. That which lies at the end of history had been experienced in history, and Jesus was perceived as the doorway through which one goes from one realm to the other. He is the door, the way, the life; no one comes to the Father but by him—that is the way the Fourth Gospel finally said it.

That risen Christ was real. I cannot say that too emphatically. He was not resuscitated, he was *resurrected*. He was changed. It was not the limited physical eyes of our humanity that saw him, but eyes of faith newly opened by the power of his life—but those newly opened eyes really saw him. This was no mirage, no vision, no hallucination. There is no vocabulary, no language of the eschatological realm; so we have to use our inadequate human language. Resurrection cannot be explained or narrated. It can only be experienced and proclaimed. Death cannot contain him. He lives.

It was obvious, I suspect, to the other dinner guests that something had happened to Peter. He stopped talking. He stood as if in a trance with a piece of the broken loaf in each hand. For Peter it must have seemed as if an eternity had passed. To the others at the table perhaps it was only an instant, an eerie kind of instant. Then Peter, suddenly aglow with life, turned back to the table and led them step by step through the broken bread to look anew at the cross and then into the experience of their own resurrection and finally to open their eyes to see the resurrected Jesus.

There was an intensity about that Moment that burned all fear and cowardice out of the disciples. They had entered that room as fugitives in hiding. They would leave that room as transformed, fearless, resurrected men who would start a movement that would transform the world. That Moment had captured a reality that would forever stamp the day when that Moment would be reenacted as a special day, forever holy; for on that day followers of Jesus would meet and break bread together and experience his living presence again and again. So a new holy day was born.

Finally, when Jesus was seen, when the power of his life was experienced, when the realm beyond history broke into their consciousnesses, suddenly Jesus and God were seen as a single reality. He was both the servant of God who took upon himself the brokenness of the creation, was victimized by it, and vindicated through it; but he was also the Son of Man who would inaugurate the dawn of the new age when God would be all in all. Now they looked back at his life, his words, his actions, and they understood. Jesus is Lord, they exclaimed. It was the first and maybe the best Christian creed. They worshiped him, an unheard-of thing for Jewish people to do. "My Lord and my God" is the ecstatic cry that captures the impact of this revolution. Never again could they envision God without including in that definition Jesus the Christ. Never again could they think of Jesus without seeing him as included in all that the word *God* meant.

When the disciples stepped into the Moment of Easter led by Peter, the Spirit that had *conceived* this Jesus entered them. The love, the power, the fullness of life was theirs. The Spirit was the same as Jesus and yet different. John described it as "Jesus breathed on them, and they received the Holy Spirit." It was all part of the Moment of Easter. Luke later for rational and apologetic reasons would separate the various *movements* of the Easter Moment, but at first it was one cascading, revelatory encounter with life at a depth never before experienced. They saw all that life could be, both in history and beyond history or, in the traditional language, both on earth and in heaven. And Jesus the giver and source of that life clearly belonged to both realms. The God–man they came to call him, ascended to heaven yet present on earth through the Holy Spirit.

Peter and whoever shared that Easter Moment with him now left Jerusalem and returned to Galilee to locate the other disciples to bring them into the Easter Moment. They found them, and in Galilee once more they saw the Lord. The disciple band was reconstituted, and they began to understand that the Easter Moment was not a privilege but a responsibility. They must *feed my sheep*. Freely they had received; freely they must give. They knew dimensions of life into which they wanted to invite others. They knew a depth of community that overcame all the human barriers—language, class, tribe, race. They were citizens of a new creation. In Jesus they were given life in all its fullness, open, honest, risking, free. They shared in the New Being which they had found in Jesus. And this New Being must be given away.

The Easter Moments in Galilee all seem to have this imperative quality. Matthew has the risen Lord give the divine commission: "Go into all the world—Judea, Samaria, the uttermost parts of the earth. Be my witnesses, baptize in my name. Lo, I am with you always to the end of time." The words are clearly stylized, theologized, polished. But the dawning of a worldwide responsibility for those who had seen the living Lord was not to be denied.

Obviously at some point the disciples, including those who had fled to Galilee, gathered again in Jerusalem. It was in Jerusalem that the Christian movement burst upon the public. That gathering was clearly one of ecstatic joy. That day could well have been remembered as the birthday of the church, and it could well have possessed the qualities of Pentecost. This may be the historic event that underlies Luke's story of the coming of the Holy Spirit, and Luke, knowing that this was sometime after the Easter Moment, adjusted his chronology to fit his understanding of this event.

Whatever lies behind the narrative, it is clear that the Easter Moment, which included Resurrection, Ascension, and the Holy Spirit, also carried with it a missionary imperative. The obligation to follow and to share the resurrected one are both inherent in having the eyes to see. The reality of the event and the significance of the event are indivisible.

Everywhere the Christians went, they told the story of their living Lord. They shared his love. They invited men and women into the experience of Easter, interpreting it with the symbols of broken bread and poured-out wine. Here was the context of Easter. Here successive generations could meet the living Lord and know the love that sets life free to be, to live, to love, to risk. The breaking of bread became *the* liturgical act for Christians, *the* meeting place with the resurrected Lord of life. Inevitably, just as with the Easter Moment, to proclaim this Eucharistic act as the meeting place with the Lord of life was not sufficient. It had to be narrated, explained, rationalized, and defended.

It was not long before theories abounded as to just how the Lord was present in this experience. Transubstantiation, consubstantiation, memorial meals, and that marvelously vague and typically Anglican view called *the Real Presence* are the modern names of the rational explanations. Like the narrations and explanations of the Easter Moment, the language, the vocabulary, the mind-set are all inadequate. They can only point to what they so ineptly try to describe. But that will not prevent men and women from arguing endlessly over their interpretations, even to the point of rending asunder the body of Christ to defend their version of the truth. And the Holy God must smile at the constant folly of those he loves and for whom that love was shown in the cross of Calvary.

That is how I would reconstruct the Moment of Easter. It is real for me, real beyond imagining. It is not a moment that can be measured by the scientist or by the historian, for its reality is beyond the domain of either discipline. But that does not mean that that Moment is not real. It only means that science and history have not exhausted all that is real. It means that life has a depth, a transcendence, that most of us never touch.

I look at Jesus, my Lord, and I see a life that reveals the source of all life. I see a love that reveals the source of all love. I see being that reveals the ground of all being. Since God is for me that personal center of the universe that is life, love, and being, I see God when I look at Jesus. But more than that I see what life can be beyond our brokenness, our fragmentation, our ego needs, our defense systems, our security barriers. In Jesus I meet God and a vision of complete and whole humanity calling me to dare to risk my own security by entering life, knowing another, being known, loving another, being loved, being myself without apology, without boasting, and allowing others to be themselves.

When the depth of a relationship is experienced, when true community is found, the same transforming, transcending reality touches life and calls each of us to grasp a new being. When one stands here, he or she cannot help looking anew at Jesus and understanding. Yes, he died, but he was more alive dying than those around him were living. And he touched life so deeply that in his power all of the barriers, even the barrier of death, melted away. That seems to me always to happen when real life is met, engaged, shared. At some point depth becomes transcendence, and death is seen as the gateway to life.

I shared with my readers in the opening part of this volume my experience with one of the people of God. His name was Jim Campbell. I am alive today in a way I could never have been had he not allowed me to share in all that his life meant, including the incident of his death. I do not mean to trivialize that death, for in many ways it was traumatic for Jim, for his wife, for his son, and for his daughter. In a unique way it was traumatic for me. But nonetheless it was but an incident, for when he died, Jim was alive in a new way. And death could not touch that life.

There is another realm. Jesus entered it. He opened eyes to see it. I have experienced it. Many of you have also, though perhaps you do not always know how to articulate what it is you have experienced. Love gives life. Love expands being. Love opens eyes to new dimensions. Love leads us toward a completion of ourselves. In that process it is not hard to see the one who was fully alive, fully loving, fully being who he was, also to be the risen, life-giving spirit, and beckoning us to come to him, to share in his peace that passes all understanding—and I might add, all human categories of language.

Death could not and cannot contain him. Jesus lives. Jesus is Lord. Broken bread revealed and reveals him. Surely I am a skeptical child of a nonbelieving twentieth century. But on this truth I gladly wager my very life. I stand here unashamed, unembarrassed. For me the Easter Moment is truth. Truth I can enter. Truth I have entered. Truth I will more fully enter. For now I see through a glass darkly, but someday face to face.

Because I believe this, I am committed to living as fully as possible now in this moment, in every moment. I am willing to reveal myself and to allow others to trust me with revelations of themselves. I am committed to a life of risk, of love, of relationships, of honesty. The hope of heaven can never be an excuse not to live now. It must always be rather an invitation to live now, a challenge to be myself now. For I am a disciple of the one who said, "I have come that you might have life, abundantly, here and hereafter."

Part IV

Entering the
Easter Moment

Chapter 19

The Eucharist

At the center of the Christian Church's life is the eucharistic act of breaking bread. This worship act goes by many names: Eucharist, the Lord's Supper, the Mass, Holy Communion, Divine Liturgy, just to name a few. It has been the subject of various explanations, theologies, apologetics. It is a major point of discussion in every ecumenical conversation. The Eucharist has been used by the church and by churchpeople as a means to divide the ins from the outs, as a privilege of membership in the *true church* from which all who are not members of the true church are excluded. These barriers are breaking down, but they still exist and sometimes result in both pain and embarrassment.

The ability to lead Eucharist or to say the mass has been the source of enormous power in the priesthood, which power has been jealously guarded from outsiders and heightened with all sorts of ritual acts to lend mystery and wonder to the liturgy. Even the act of cleansing the vessels after the Eucharist is in many traditions highly stylized and filled with numerous symbols that bespeak a typically human literalization of the symbols. As long as there are men and women of different temperaments, different emotional and religious needs, each possessing a different intellectual grasp of reality, there will be different interpretations of this eucharistic act.

I certainly do not want to play the game of what is best or right or true. Rather, I would prefer to affirm all of these approaches for a moment as liturgical acts that always point beyond themselves to a truth or a reality that they can never capture. Heresy is not found in an inadequate eucharistic theology nearly so much as it is found in the literalization of any eucharistic symbol. To confuse the reality pointed to with the pointer is to misunderstand the whole meaning of a sacrament. My advice and my hope would be that each Christian and each Christian tradition would explore the meaning of their understanding of this liturgical act as deeply, reverently, and experientially as possible. At the end of every understanding there will always be a mystery that words cannot embrace but hearts cannot doubt.

My thesis in this volume has attempted to relate the Easter Moment to the eucharistic act in a way that makes one almost nonsensical without the other. The liturgical act of breaking bread in memory of Jesus became the event that opened the disciples' eyes to the meaning of Jesus and the truth of his living, resurrected presence beyond the fact of his death. Easter forever stamped the eucharistic action of breaking bread in memory of him as the historic meeting place between the believer and his/her living Lord. There was an objectivity about this action and about the experience of Christ in this action that resisted the romantic, subjective rhetoric of later pietism.

Now I would like to take my readers behind the words, the theologies, the explanations of the Eucharist into the experience itself, which I suggest is nothing less than the experience of Easter. I will do this not by following the outline of any particular eucharistic tradition but by focusing on the main components of every eucharistic act. (These are generally agreed to be six in number.) The people gather, the Gospel is read and expounded, the prayers are offered, the peace is exchanged, the Eucharist is made and shared, and the dismissal is given.

Eucharist must begin with a gathering. Lives must come together. We always come out of many backgrounds, carrying many agendas. Each of us lives and loves in some human constellation—a family, a staff, a commune, a community. When we gather, different things are happening, being remembered, threatening, being celebrated in each constellation by each person— birthdays, anniversaries of marriages and of deaths, moments of victory and defeat, community and loneliness, excitement and fear, fulfillment and threat, alienation and forgiveness, involvement and retreat—these constitute the stuff of our humanity, and inevitably we bring our humanity with us when we gather to worship. It is important to be aware of who we are and of where we are and who others are and from what direction they are coming. Life has many tributaries, and some of them we must travel alone; but those tributaries must flow together sometime. Eucharistic worship is such a time.

A radical honesty must mark a gathered community that is conscious of being in the presence of the one "unto whom all hearts are open, all desires known and from whom no secrets are hid." Here we cannot pretend, and here we do not need to pretend. We are called simply to be. Our masks are lowered, our being is exposed. It is scary. We do not like to be vulnerable. We feel so weak, so defenseless. So much of our energy is directed toward hiding behind defense systems that protect our status or defend our security. We struggle to wrap our lives in the clothes of acceptability. We really do not want to be known very deeply; for we know ourselves, and most of us do not like what we know. "I'm not OK," we say to ourselves in the words of Thomas Harris. Should anyone know us as well as we know ourselves, they would not like us either, we fear.

So we hide and yet we gather, and others who are also scared gather. The power present in gathered people is astonishing and so is the fear, so are the defense systems. The gathered folk hear the demands of the Creator and all-knowing God. Love God; love your neighbor; love yourself. But I do not; I cannot; I cannot be what I was created to be, whole, free, and full. I am not giving; I am grasping. I am not content to be; rather, I am always struggling to become. We gather as we are; we confront the vision of what we were created to be. And so we hear ourselves saying, "Kyrie Eleison—Lord have mercy." That is penitence.

Then the Gospel is read and proclaimed. It tells the astonishing good news that we are loved, accepted, forgiven, "just as we are without one plea." The whole meaning of Jesus' life is proclaimed in the Gospel. On the other side of Easter when these books were written, his teaching is seen to be a full disclosure of the meaning of his life. To be embraced by this love is to enter the kingdom of heaven, to be united with your own deepest destiny. It is to possess the pearl of great price, to hear the divine *well done,* to be welcomed as the prodigal by the loving Father. The mighty acts of healing are illustrative of what love can do in human life, restoring, recalling, recreating wholeness of body, mind, and spirit. The drama of Jesus' passion is now seen as he intended it: a proclamation by this solitary life that nothing we can be or do can separate us from the love of God, for even when we crucify the love of God, his response is to love us still. That is the Gospel we hear, and it speaks to the very depths of our being, and it looses in us a call to life that must be answered. It challenges our shallowness, our superficiality, our one-dimensional existence.

We have to respond. Gospel demands that. We say yes in creeds, in prayers, in offerings of ourselves, our substance, our stewardship of God's creation. We bring our concerns, our pain, our joy, our brokenness, our hope, our money, our bread and wine. It is all we have. But we would not offer it if we did not know already that it is acceptable. In our prayers we stretch our vision and escape our narrow orbit of concern. To approach the Holy God is to embrace his creation. We know more about this today than previous generations have known, for ours is a tiny spaceship planet called Earth, radically interdependent. War anywhere is really a civil war, dividing the one family of God's creation. Those anywhere who despoil the environment despoil our common home. Those who violate the rights and dignity of any human being distort the image of God in every human being. So in our prayers we roam the edges of our human experience and lift it to God without neglecting our own deepest and most personal concerns. We do not know how, but we do know that God's loving embrace holds all we love. So guard, heal, protect, be with my child, my wife, my husband, my parent, my friend. If we did not pray that way, we would not be honest. And so we do.

Then we share the peace. We acknowledge one another as part of a human community gathered in worship. We affirm, we touch, we greet, we share. We seek to give that which frees another to be himself or herself: the peace of Christ. We are not alone; we are part of a family. We need others; others need us. How humbling, how mighty, how freeing. The load seems lighter when we touch another life and when another life touches us. Fear recedes, community grows, peace descends.

Then the eucharistic act begins. The table is prepared. Bread and wine are presented, symbols of God's creation. The ancient words are recited. The first Easter is reenacted. The ordained leader is Peter, not Christ, seeking to open our eyes. "For on the night in which he was betrayed, he took bread. When he had given thanks, he broke it and said, 'Take, eat. This is my body broken for you.' Likewise he took the cup, again gave thanks, and shared it. 'Drink this all of you. This is my blood of the New Covenant. This do in remembrance of me.' For as oft as you eat this bread and drink this cup you show forth the Lord's death until he comes."

We hear! We enter that Moment. We stretch out empty hands, and they are filled. We look beyond the limits of our sight, and we see; for we are met, accepted, loved, forgiven, resurrected. We are called into a new being, and the calling one who always stands before us is the living Lord. "Come unto me. I will give you rest." Rest from the eternal human struggle to become. Rest that is not static resignation but the dynamic acceptance of the fullness of our own being. We can know this rest when the barriers that we erect to protect our being are broken. Such barriers always stifle our life. They never protect our life.

Our being finally needs no security systems, no ego crutches, no tribal, national, or racial definitions. It only needs to be allowed to live, to stretch, to grow. Here in this eucharistic act our being is freed, transformed, expanded, and suddenly there are no limits. Not even death can abort the potential of our humanity. We have met the Lord, and we are changed. We receive him. His life enters our life. The eternal Easter enters the present now. Jesus could not be contained in a tomb. Easter cannot be contained in a moment of past history. It is beyond history, metahistorical but real. Here inside this eucharistic moment it does not occur to us to debate the point. We just proclaim it, and those who want to understand must be invited into the experience, for it is beyond words, beyond theology, beyond liturgy.

We say our thanksgivings. Blessed by the presence and peace of the risen Christ, we are dismissed. We rise to reenter that world where humanity is violated, where scared people grasp for power, where death is omnipresent. In that world we become the salt of the earth, giving life a savor it otherwise would not have. We become leaven in the lump, working to expand life, to lighten the loads of injustice. We become a small flickering light in the darkness, a light that gives hope, that announces that the darkness shall not extinguish hope. That witness takes many forms. Sometimes it is a personal example, a quiet word, a simple act. Sometimes it is a powerful protest, a peace-shattering demonstration that shakes the political establishment. In God's economy both are important, both are needed.

We are dismissed to witness to the Resurrection of our Lord in all kinds of ways. Sometimes the witness is effective. Sometimes it is defeated. Sometimes it is costly. Our task is to be faithful, not to be successful. We are to lift him up. He must draw all people to himself in his own way. It is not for us to judge how anyone else lifts him up. That is the stuff of religious bigotry. It is our task simply to witness. The dismissal is nothing less than our version of the words Matthew puts into the mouth of the risen Christ in Galilee. Go into all the world. Preach. Baptize. I am with you always. Go in peace to love and serve the Lord. We respond, "Thanks be to God."

We gather, we disperse. That is the rhythm of life, of faith, of Easter. All of this lies under the eucharistic act performed in the great cathedrals with pomp and circumstance or at a bedside with a young doctor dying of leukemia or in a country church where simple people with sunburned faces and dirt-stained hands proclaim their profound earthiness or in an office where a staff gathers to offer their work to God. It is the meeting place with the Lord of life. In that meeting place we always hear the eternal call of the Gospel of Christ. It is a call to dare, to live, to love, to risk, to be.

We enter it. And when we do, we move beyond words into life, life that knows no barrier, not even the barrier of death.

Chapter 20

Life after Death

I f there is no resurrection of the dead, then Christ has not been raised and our faith is in vain." This was Paul's way of spelling out the relationship between Jesus' Resurrection and our own resurrections. If Jesus is the first fruits of them that sleep, then we who are in Christ live in hope of our own participation in resurrection and in life after death.

In this concluding chapter I want to be very specific. I believe in a personal life after death. I believe in it deeply and consciously. I am not embarrassed or apologetic about that conviction even in this skeptical, nonbelieving twentieth century in which I am also a devoted citizen.

When one talks about life after death, it is particularly easy to be phony. I hope to avoid that. Above all else, I want to be honest theologically. I want to share only what I can in honest conviction state that I believe. I do not want simply to parrot the traditions and pretend that they still have power for me if they do not. But I also want to respect those traditions at least to the extent that I will probe underneath the literal words trying to discern the issues those words were created to convey. Then if that inner reality I discover beyond those words still has validity and power, I want to find new words that for my age and my time will carry the meaning that yesterday's words carried for yesterday's world. In this process I believe that I must not hesitate boldly to set aside words and images that no longer have meaningful content for me or my day. Most of the language that purports to speak of life after death for me falls in this category.

Hell, for example, carries no content whatever for our generation. It is an empty mild oath. Even its literal content is violated, for on a blustery winter day, one frequently hears such phrases as "It's cold as hell today." The same person will call a blistering summer day "hot as hell."

Heaven has an equally vague content in our day as an analysis of the contemporary uses of that word and concept in the English language will reveal. I notice with great interest that adults are much more prone to talk glibly about heaven to children who have experienced the death of a loved one than they are when talking to bereaved adults. Recently, a well-known sports hero was tragically killed in an airplane crash. He was thirty-two. He had been known as a devoted family man who was very close to his children. According to the newspaper account his widow, trying to comfort her children, talked about the beauties of heaven and how great an honor it was for Daddy to be wanted by God so badly that God took him so early. One of the young children, noting the disparity between these words and the behavior of the mourners that he was observing, was quoted as saying, "If Dad is so lucky, why is everyone crying?" The honesty of children punctures the sentimentality and phoniness of adults time after time. What is revealed about what we really believe when we use *heaven talk* primarily with children and not with our peers?

Look at other cultural uses of the word heaven. There are such things as the innumerable *St. Peter at the gate* jokes. There are romantic ballads that proclaim "I'm in heaven when I'm with you." There are special places of beauty or meaning that we exaggerate by likening them to heaven. My undergraduate university was in Chapel Hill, North Carolina, a place known to its alumni as *the southern part of heaven.* When a lemon meringue pie is described as *heavenly,* the emptiness of the word is particularly, even painfully, apparent.

The reason heaven and hell have no believable, recognizable content today comes from the fact that archaic and meaningless symbols have been attached to these words. These symbols were first literalized, and when these literalizations were not able to grow and change, they inevitably became sillier and sillier to people until finally they became jokes that were first funny and then embarrassing. I know of no one who is drawn to the heavenly vision of *a land flowing with milk and honey, a place of golden streets and lampstands,* or even *a place of eternal rest.* The concept identified with the book of Revelation ("a place where there is no sorrow or sadness, no persecution or separation") may still have some appeal, but it is certainly not of the magnitude that it once was.

In terms of the nethermost regions of hell, I know of few people who are afraid of a literal devil complete with tail and pitchfork. I am certainly neither frightened nor motivated by visions of fiery pits and brimstone and eternal torment. I do not believe that even so eloquent a preacher as Jonathan Edwards could get a hearing today for his famous "sinners in the hands of an angry God" sermon with which he brought about the *great awakening* on the American frontier in the eighteenth century. The image of God dangling sinners by the singed hairs of their heads over the flames of hell would not capture much today beyond comic relief. Because the content of the symbols has lost meaning and power, the symbols themselves have fallen into disuse and disrepute. If the symbols of heaven and hell are to be redeemed, a new content that is in touch with our life's experience must be found.

The first task in this reclamation project is to get beneath the literal words past generations have applied to these symbols and examine the meaning they had in the context of the lives of the people who produced that content.

A land flowing with milk and honey comes out of the Old Testament and was originally a concept applied to Canaan, which to the wilderness-wandering Israelites was *the promised land.* It is not hard to understand how under the impact of the Christian Church our life here on earth became identified with *the wilderness experience* and our entry into heaven became *the promised land.* But originally the promised land was understood in terms of how the people of Israel experienced their need. The wilderness was rugged. Survival was always an issue. Food supplies were always insecure. There were no supermarkets, freezers, or chemical fertilizers to guarantee an abundant crop. Fulfillment, joy, peace was to have that anxiety of hunger removed, and so they dreamed of a land flowing with milk and honey.

The promised land became, not surprisingly, a utopian existence where their needs were met.

Golden streets and lampstands were, of course, symbols of wealth that people in poverty believed would bring fulfillment. The content, I am sure, came from the city of Jerusalem, which was called the Golden City and was for the people of Israel the symbol of wealth and success. No one who has ever seen Jerusalem from a distance high on its impregnable hill with the golden rays of the setting sun illumining it with a lustre and a brilliance that literally lifts it out of the desert background and gives it an unearthly sparkle and splendor will ever wonder how it was that *Jerusalem the golden* or *the new Jerusalem* became a symbol of heavenly bliss.

The eternal rest symbol likewise grew out of human need. In feudal Europe and later in slave America and in pre-union industrialized nations, it was the lot of serfs or slaves and workers to labor at backbreaking toil six days out of every week from sunup to sundown. By this time the Christian holy day Sunday had been merged to some degree with the Jewish Sabbath. Hence, Sunday was the day of rest, the only day when the serfs or slaves or workers were not forced to work. So the day of rest became the yearned-for day, enjoyed above all others. It was never long enough. Monday with its renewed toil always came too soon. So quite naturally people began to picture heaven as the eternal sabbath of rest, where the burdens of our labor could be put aside and we could enter into the blessed and deserved rest promised to faithful servants.

The Revelation picture of heaven also had an historic context. That book of the Bible was written during a period of intense persecution. It was the common lot of Christians to be arrested, imprisoned, executed.

Families were separated. Loved ones were thrown in jail, fed to lions, burned at the stake. So quite naturally they dreamed of heaven in terms of the deepest need that they were experiencing. Heaven was conceived of in terms of a place where there is no sorrow, no sadness, no persecution, no separation or death.

When the content of heaven is analyzed in each of these instances, when we sink beneath the level of literalism, one fact becomes both obvious and consistent. All of the content we use to describe heaven represents the way we experience fulfillment or the overcoming of our primary sense of need at that particular moment in time and history. So underneath the literal content, heaven is always a hope, a dream, a yearning for that which completes or fulfills our life. Our task is to understand how we experience incompleteness today and to seek to frame the content of that word heaven which means fulfillment in such a way as to have it stand for our deepest hope, our fondest dream. Then we will reach the edge of the final theological question any life can ask, namely, is God real to us because God is real, or is God real to us because we need God to be real and therefore create God to meet our own needs? Or to frame that question in terms of this discussion, do we create our heaven, our place of fulfillment, because of our need for fulfillment; or does our incompleteness drive us toward that reality for which we were created, from which we are now separated, and for which we legitimately yearn? How we answer that question will determine the way we approach any theological issue, indeed any life issue.

It is my conviction that life must be entered fully and deeply before we will have the experience and the data that would cause us to bet our lives totally and without

reservation on the reality of God and the trustwor-
thiness of heaven. Note please that the historic content
of the word heaven points far more to the quality of
life than to the quantity of life. Many people I have
known have found length of days to be anything but
satisfying and fulfilling, and the prospect of an eternity
of time would fill their lives with fear and despair. My
relationship with Jim Campbell taught me that eternal
life is not found in endless time. Rather eternal life is
discovered when one dares to risk depth, to enter life,
to plunge into the very core of oneself and others.
There one finds transcendence, timelessness, eternity.
It is not longevity; it is depth.

With that insight I was able to look again at the Resurrection of my Lord Jesus Christ and see the intensity
of his life, his ability to live fully, to love completely, to
be all that he was created to be. He was able to risk everything, to give himself away totally, and to enable the
disciples to see in these qualities a doorway into eternity. God was revealed in Jesus at these points when
life was affirmed, love was shared, and time possessed
eternal meaning. The disciples entered this experience,
and when they did, *they* were resurrected; then their
eyes were opened and they saw Jesus. Resurrection
meant not only that Jesus was alive, but also that he
was one with God. He was the doorway to God, opening to all and inviting all to come, enter, live, love, be,
and experience the timelessness of heaven. So this is
the clue that I must grasp in order to approach, to
believe in, or to enter what lies behind the word
heaven.

All of us have experienced to some degree and in
some measure the reality of human joy. For me the
deepest experience of human joy is in an honest and

loving human relationship. I am a privileged man. I know what it means to love and to be loved. I know the warmth of a friend, the fulfillment of honest meeting. I know the peace and the pleasure that comes from sharing life with another. I know the power that is present when one life reveals its true being and another life accepts and embraces that revelation. I know what it means to trust and be trusted, to care and to be cared for, to forgive and to be forgiven. These are the richest and the deepest moments of life for me; and it is in these moments that I catch a glimpse of life's true meaning, of life's endless depth, of life's infinite potential.

Yet even as sweet and affirming as these moments are, they only point beyond themselves. They are but glimpses into life's fullness and life's perfection. They never capture it or exhaust it. Life is always bigger than anything I have yet experienced. Life teaches me that the more deeply I live, the more fulfillment I experience, the more my life is filled with an even greater hope. This hope proclaims that what I glimpse here and now, what I experience at the very heart and core of life in these my deepest moments of meaning are but fleeting pointers to what can be, what shall be, and to what my human destiny really is.

To live fully, to love totally, to be set free to be completely myself—this is my hope, my deepest human yearning. It is the quest for this reality that motivates me to invest my life recklessly in human relationships. It is the joy of this investment that opens my eyes and compels me to believe that the meaning I taste here that bubbles up in the very heart of life's deepest meetings is an unending reality. It is a doorway into an eternity where finally life's yearnings are satisfied, the taste is filled, and hopes are realized. In this way I can be whole, complete, at one with another, with God, and with myself. For me, this is the content that fills the word heaven.

Its opposite makes this definition even more obvious, for I, like each one who reads these words, also know what it means to be hurt, to be misunderstood, to be alienated, to be alone, to be outside the forgiveness of a friend. I know what it means to ache in a broken relationship. I know the pain that comes when life is denied, when rejection kills, when hurt drives me more deeply into the shell of my own insecurity. I know what it means to lash back in defensiveness and watch the rift widen. I have on more than one occasion been forced to live in isolation from a friend who once had been meaning and life to me. This kind of personal hurt is the most exquisite torture that life possesses. It is out of these hurtful experiences that I can imagine and even feel something of what absolute loneliness must be.

Separation from love is an unbearable reality, for it is a denial of life. The separated lonely one inevitably turns inward, nurses his or her own wounds, seeks to meet his or her own needs, and soon exhausts his or her reserves. If the separation is profound enough, it will weaken all ties to all others. If these ties ever cease to exist, personhood shrivels and dies. Since God is the source of life and love and the ground of being for me, then one separated from life, love, and being is finally separated from God. Beyond fiery pits, brimstone, devils, which are nothing but literalized attempts to describe the deepest human pain, there is hell. But anyone who has ever lived knows full well that the deepest human pain is never physical; it is rather always the pain of being separated from meaning, from love, from relationships, from God. Hell is the absence of meaning, the destruction of life, the loneliness of isolation. Hell is real. To some degree, in some measure, everyone who lives or has lived has been there. Perhaps it is not so much an eternal abode as it has been traditionally pictured as it is nothingness, darkness, extermination, death.

God is love. This simple and yet profound definition was shaped first by St. John who went on to say that whoever abides in love abides in God. To be loved, says our human experience, is to be alive. To be loved is to see our being expand. Only in the process of being loved do we experience the expansion and the sweetness of life. Yet the deepest love that we experience in our human relationships is still inadequate, still incomplete. The paradox of life is that the more we experience of life, the more we know there is to experience. The deeper we plunge into being, the more vast we discover is the potential living possesses. No matter how fulfilling any moment of life is, it is only a foretaste, a teasing sample of what life can be. Every sample creates in us a more insatiable hunger that makes us both hope and yearn for that perfect love which issues in total life. This in turn points us both into life and beyond life where this yearning will finally be satisfied. Some of us in the rare privileged moments of life have been up on the mountaintop where we have seen what is beyond. It is real. At the heart of life one meets love that is transcendent, and this love grasps us, and before it every finite barrier fades. Yes, even the barrier of death is overcome.

This love was the secret of Jesus' life, and when men and women entered that secret, they knew that death could not contain him. With eyes that pierced the curtain of finite history, they saw him risen, transcendent, resurrected. I trust this reality. In this hope and confidence I live. Jesus' Resurrection reveals my ultimate destiny and yours. It is nothing less than the fullness of life which flows into eternity. I am finally but a stranger here, a wanderer, a pilgrim; heaven is my home.

How then do I prepare for dying? It is not by pious activity, I can assure you, but rather by daring to live, by having the courage to be all I am capable of being, by risking all that I am and all that I have in human relationships. I prepare for death by allowing myself to be known, by trusting others with my life, by opening myself to all of the possibilities of loving and caring. This means that I am willing to become vulnerable to hurt by venturing out of my security shell into the real arenas of life. In this manner of living, my faith bids me to prepare for death. Death is finally overcome not by fleeing it and not by truncating or running away from life. Rather it is overcome by plunging to life's core, risking all in the reckless gamble of loving vulnerability and discovering at life's center the secret that opens the doors to timelessness, fullness, perfect love, heaven.

This was the secret of Jesus' life that exploded the consciousness of the disciples and opened their eyes in the Moment of Easter. This was the Moment when they knew that God and Jesus were not separable. This was the Moment when they were compelled to worship the resurrected one who was the way, the truth, and the life. That door is still open to us, for the Easter Moment is a moving phenomenon not limited by time or space or history. A life lived in the power of this

Christ knows that even the sting of death can be overcome and the darkness of the grave will not finally be victorious.

So let us live deeply, fully, richly, and venturing all that we are in the ever-deepening discovery that to spend life is to possess life, to waste love is to have love. Let us dare to touch and feel and give and trust until we enter another life's very being. Plunging into the very depth of human relationships is the doorway to the fullness of life. There life will be met in all its fullness, life that I believe transcends every human barrier—yes, even time and space and death.

Chapter 21

A Concluding Word

By this time my reader has journeyed quite a distance with me.

We began by trying to understand the limitation of words, the subjectivity of language, the historic conditioning of the minds with which each of us tries to understand the mystery of the world about us. We explored some intensely human experiences that seemed to have been invested with eternity. Then we looked anew at Jesus of Nazareth, the life through which we Christians assert we have met that awe, mystery, wonder, and love we call God. The moment that surely stands at the interpretive center of that life is the Easter Moment; so there we focused.

That Moment had enormous effects in history, which effects we sought to identify and to measure without trying to prove too much. Something occurred that changed lives, reconstituted a scattered band, energized discouraged, cowardly men, removed fear, reoriented family prejudices, gave birth to a new holy day, and changed dramatically a concept of God so as to include within it Jesus of Nazareth called the Christ. The effects are in history. For the cause we must look beyond history.

We studied the biblical narratives that purport to deal with this Moment and we analyzed the world view of the first-century Jewish mind for clues as to how that which was beyond history could somehow be experienced in time by historic people. We explored many clues. We found abundant evidence that the sharing of food, the breaking of bread, seems to be at the heart of the early narrations about the Moment of Easter.

Throughout this pilgrimage, we walked the razor's edge of human language, trying to find words that did not distort the experience that clearly words cannot capture. Easter is objective. Easter is subjective. Easter is both objective and subjective. Easter is neither objective nor subjective. Easter is beyond objectivity or subjectivity. All are true; all are inadequate.

To literalize the accounts of Easter is to destroy it. Not to literalize the experience of Easter is to distort it. Easter is real, eternal, nonhistoric, ever available. We carried our search to the point where, at least for me, a truth emerges that my words cannot penetrate, a Moment my concepts cannot capture, but a Moment my heart cannot doubt. So I too proclaim, death cannot contain him. Jesus lives.

This Lord Jesus is worthy of the attention of this century and of the worship of those of us who inhabit this moment in time. The Eternal Easter enters the present now. We look to the Easter Moment to hear its call to life, to love, and to the courage to be all that God created us to be. This is the power that Jesus revealed, the power he lived, the power he was and is.

"He is not here," they said.
"He is Risen."
Christpower.
As it was in the beginning,
it is now,
And so shall it ever be.[18]

For your willingness to share this pilgrimage with me, I offer my thanks. May your life know the peace and love of Christ.

Shalom.

Notes

1. The Chalcedonian formula was produced by the Council of Chalcedon in A.D. 451 and is generally regarded as settling for all time the conflict between the humanity of Jesus and the divinity of Jesus: "recognized in two natures, without confusion, without change, without division, without separation, the distinction of natures being in no way annulled by the Union."

2. Temporary remissions have been known in the disease, but they have always been of short duration.

3. This is the title of one of Dr. Paul Tillich's great works.

4. This point is defended by Prof. Hans Kung in his book *On Being a Christian*.

5. The most exhaustive analysis of the role and myth of Mary in Western church life is found in Marina Warner's work, *Alone of All Her Sex*.

6. A much more complete treatment of this development can be found in Chapter 7 of my book *The Living Commandments* (New York: Seabury Press, 1977).

7. The reader may be interested to know that Hosea 11:1 and Matthew 5:9 support this contention.

8. This is true whether these words are literal or not. Most New Testament scholars would not treat the Johannine Doubting Thomas story as history, but the fact remains that this story does complete the revolutionary thought process.

9. C. B. Moss is the author of the standard theological text used for years in many seminaries. It was a book noted for its dullness even if it attempted to encompass all theological truth.

10. Prof. Raymond Brown suggests that these verses, while not original with Mark, are in fact another early resurrection tradition, and he urges us not to dismiss them because they are not Markan. I agree with him.

11. When I say Luke, I mean not just the gospel that bears his name but also the book of Acts; together, these are generally thought to constitute the Lukan corpus.

12. There are those who believe that this transfiguration account is a misplaced resurrection narrative. If this is so, an entirely different light would be thrown upon the narrative.

13. Maurice Goguel, *La foi a la résurrection de Jésus dans la Christianisme primitif* (Paris: E. Leroux, 1933).

14. Trying to embrace this distinction, C. H. Dodd suggests that one lived inside Easter as if one had a foot in both ages.

15. The only thing that might keep this from being stated even more strongly is the Johannine hint that Jesus' baptism by John was a Judean and not a Galilean event.

16. I'm sure that if Irenaeus had lived today, he would have said, "The glory of God is man and/or woman fully alive."

17. I am deliberately treating the gospel narratives as a whole and neglecting the formal critical insights into each unit. There are many books around that will help the reader with the formal critical details. It is my hope to create a sweeping impression of the whole life without getting lost in the historicity of the formal critical details. Canonical criticism rather than form criticism is my deliberate method.

18. From John S. Spong, *Christpower*. Free verse by Lucy Newton Boswell (Richmond, Virginia: Thomas Hale Publishing Co., 1975).

Bibliography

Fuller, Reginald. *The Formation of the Resurrection Narratives.* New York: Macmillan, 1971.

Goguel, Maurice. *La foi a la résurrection de Jésus dans la Christianisme primitif.* Paris: E. Leroux, 1933.

Justin Martyr. *Dialogue with Trypho. Excerpts from the Works of St. Justin.* Edited by G. J. Davey and A. L. Williams. St. Charles, Ill.: St. Charles House, 1973.

Küng, Hans. *On Being a Christian.* Garden City, New York: Doubleday, 1976.

Loofs, Frederick. *What Is the Truth about Jesus Christ?* New York: Scribners, 1913, especially chapters 2–4.

Martelet, Gustave. *The Risen Christ and the Eucharistic World.* New York: Seabury Press, 1976.

Martin, James. *Did Jesus Rise from the Dead?* London: Lutterworth Press, 1956.

Orr, James. *The Resurrection of Jesus.* Cincinnati: Jennings and Graham, 1907.

Pannenberg, Wolfhart. *Jesus: God and Man.* Philadelphia: Westminster Press, 1968.

Perrin, Norman. *The Resurrection according to Matthew, Mark, and Luke.* Philadelphia: Fortress Press, 1977.

Ramsey, A. Michael. *The Resurrection of Christ.* Philadelphia: Westminster Press, 1956.

Schonfield, Hugh J. *The Passover Plot*. New York: Bantam Books, 1967.

Selwyn, Edward Gordon. "The Resurrection." In *Essays Catholic and Critical*. London: S.P.C.K.

Sloan, Harold Paul. *He Is Risen*. Abingdon: Cokesbury, 1952.

Spong, John Shelby. *The Living Commandments*. New York: Seabury Press, 1977.

———. *This Hebrew Lord*. New York: Seabury Press, 1974.

Warner, Marina. *Alone of All Her Sex*. New York: Knopf, 1976.

Weatherhead, Leslie D. *The Resurrection*. Abingdon: Cokesbury, 1951.

Westcott, B. F. *The Gospel of the Resurrection*. London: Macmillan, 1898.

———. *The Revelation of the Risen Lord*. London: Macmillan, 1898.

Williams, H. A. *Jesus and the Resurrection*. London: Longmans, 1951.

Yarnold, G. D. *Risen Indeed: Studies in the Lord's Resurrection*. New York: Oxford University Press, 1959.

Index